LONG JOURNEY
TO THE
ROSE GARDEN

BY JOHN TURSI & THELMA PALMER

FIDALGO BAY PUBLISHING

FIDALGO BAY PUBLISHING
ANACORTES

Cover illustration by L. Galen Larson, Galen Design

Library of Congress Cataloging-in-Publication Data
Tursi, John and Palmer, Thelma
        Long Journey to the Rose Garden
1. Biography 2. The Great Depression 3. Pacific Northwest 4. Prejudice against Italians in World War II
89-81123
ISBN 0-9624646-0-0

Printed and published in the United States of America by
Fidalgo Bay Publishing, 1160 Highway 20, Anacortes, WA 98221

Dedication

This book is affectionately dedicated to Doris Tursi and Darrell Palmer for their understanding and patience during this writing process. The delicious gourmet dinners they served at the end of each session were a great encouragement to continue the project.

John especially wishes to thank Doris for saying, "Oh, John, just go ahead and write it as it was. After all, it's been fifty years."

John Tursi, England 1942

Preface

When John Tursi first asked me to write his story, I thought it would be more work than I wished to do—even though over the many years of our friendship I had heard some of his adventures and knew they were the stuff that books are made of. One evening at a dinner party, I overheard him telling how his hunting rifles had been confiscated by the Anacortes Police Department the day after Pearl Harbor merely because he was of Italian parentage.

I was horrified at such blatant discrimination, and somewhere in the recesses of my mind, a distant memory began to come awake. A couple of days later, I remembered! I must have been about twelve years old when my mother took me into town to Doris Tursi's Kulshan Beauty Shop for my first hair appointment. I was sitting all wired up under the electric machine having my curls heated to permanence when the phone rang. As Doris hung up, I heard her say to an employee, "That was my husband. He just bought a hunting rifle." I was intrigued that I had incidentally heard about one of the rifles involved in the wartime infamy, and that made me begin paying more attention to John's stories.

When John related the story of his mother's death, I was deeply touched by the suffering of the children and shocked by the insensitivity of the mortician. I knew, then, I would write John's story for him, and though the two years I thought it would take to complete the book have stretched into three, I have not been sorry.

Along the way, I learned many fascinating details of life in Brooklyn in the twenties: how children were purged on Saturday night; how pasta was shaped into "little ears" and "seashells"; how leeches were used; how to catch a sparrow; and how water-pipe joints were soldered in the tenements. I discovered John and I share memories of Fidalgo and Whidbey Islands that go back long before we knew one another, and re-living these memories together has been a delightful journey into the past. I also learned more than I ever suspected about the myriad services that John and Doris Tursi perform quietly for our community.

Most important of all, I learned much about the resilience of the human heart and how goodness can grow out of inauspicious beginnings. I re-learned what my Scandinavian parents taught me, that hard work and determination do pay off, and it is still possible to pull yourself up by the bootstraps in America.

The Tursis share with others, working tirelessly at the Soroptimist Thrift Shop helping to earn the money that the Soroptimists use for scholarships and other projects. They are deeply involved with the Skagit County Historical Museum, and worked for years with the Anacortes Historical Museum, John using his building skills as well as his historical knowlege. Not a week passes but John volunteers to drive people who have no other means of transportation to hospitals and clinics throughout the northwest part of Washington State. He translates for Italian, French, and Spanish speaking patients at local hospitals and clinics, and teaches Italian to schoolchildren through the Mentor Program.

After John's retirement from Shell Oil Company, the Tursis became inveterate travelers, journeying into China, Japan, Tibet, and India as well as throughout western Europe. They share slides of these travels with local religious, service and senior groups, having presented literally hundreds of shows.

Throughout the writing of this book, I have tried to keep the text true to John's voice and vernacular. It is his story, and I have written it almost exactly as he told it to me.

Thelma Palmer
Guemes Island, Washington
August, 1989

President Reagan was speaking to us from the steps of the White House, but I could not keep my thoughts from drifting back to family beginnings in Italy. I imagined Papa as he must have sat in his cave-dwelling at Ginzano, pondering his emigration to America. Never in his wildest dreams could he have thought that one day a son of his would be honored at the White House by the President of the United States.

John Tursi
Anacortes, Washington
August 1989

Contents

To Be of Use

The people I love the best
jump into work head first
without dallying in the shallows
and swim off with sure strokes almost out of sight.
They seem to become natives of that element,
the black sleek heads of seals
bouncing like half-submerged balls.

I love people who harness themselves, an ox to a heavy cart,
who pull like water buffalo, with massive patience,
who strain in the mud and the muck to move things forward,
who do what has to be done, again and again.

I want to be with people who submerge
in the task, who go into the fields to harvest
and work in a row and pass the bags along,
who stand in the line and haul in their places,
who are not parlor generals and field deserters
but move in a common rhythm
when the food must come in or the fire be put out.

"To Be of Use" from *Circles on the Water*
by Marge Piercy, copywright © 1982
Reprinted by permission of Alfred A. Knopf, Inc.

1

First Memories, Mostly About Mama

A Guest to Whom We May Not Speak and a Funeral Procession

"*E mia casa,*" Mama shouted. It was her house, and she did not want to share it. Particularly with any mysterious stranger.

Her words, directed to my oldest brother, Antonio, flew over my head. I sat on the linoleum floor pulling on my first lace-up shoes, eagerly anticipating Tommy Chevi's funeral procession. Mama told me Tommy was going to be buried today. He had been well-liked by everyone on our block, and I had wakened early—as excited as if I were going to Father Appo's to eat Eucharist-wafer leftovers and stack pennies. Tommy's funeral was going to be outstanding.

First would come the brass band in their black short-billed caps and high-collared jackets; then the casket (Tommy's would be flag-draped!) in a horse-drawn hearse; next the mourners on foot; and, finally, the open touring cars filled with sprays and wreaths. The number of "flower-cars" always indicated how high up the social or criminal ladder the dead person had climbed, so we boys counted very carefully as they passed.

Tommy Chevi had returned to Brooklyn after World War I and moved in with his parents, a good Italian family across from us on 65th Street. He had served in the Navy and, like most immigrant kids who had no trade, he was attracted to the dangerous life and big money of the gangsters. Frankie Yale lived three blocks away and his gang was currently battling a rival Chicago gang that wanted to control the booze racket in New York as well as Chicago, so Yale needed a bodyguard. He hired Tommy for the job, making him not only bodyguard but chauffeur as well, and the whole neighborhood felt he had been real lucky. After all, sometimes in the bitter cold of a New York winter, Yale would have a load of coal dumped on the corner of sixty-fifth and thirteenth for anyone who needed it. People swarmed around the pile with coal scuttles, burlap sacks and buckets, and the coal quickly disappeared. One time, when his hijackers thought they were getting a load of silk, it turned out to be snow sleds and these, too, ended up on the corner so that every boy in the neighborhood was able to help himself.

Shortly after beginning his new job, Tommy drove up to the tenement where Yale lived with his wife and children. Frankie's wife saw Tommy on the street below and called out her second-story window inviting him to join them for dinner. As Tommy got out of Yale's Hupmobile sedan, another car sped by and riddled him with bullets that were probably intended for the Kingpin himself.

On this morning of Tommy's funeral, Papa had already left to harness his horse, Jim, and peddle ice down toward Borough Park; my six-year-old sister, Angelina, and my eight-year-old brother, Mike, were off to school; and I thought it was just Mama and me in our upstairs cold-flat. Then Tony came into the kitchen.

I didn't pay much attention to him because, since returning from the war in Europe, Tony seldom came home anymore. He was just a scowling shadowy figure who slipped in and out of the apartment and, on most occasions, completely ignored us, the three youngest children who had been born in America. Antonio, Pasquali and Graziano had been born in Italy and, as the eldest son, Tony became boss of the family rather than Papa because he knew English and was, therefore, better able to cope with life in Brooklyn.

My view from the floor was of their black shoes, the bottom of Mama's long black skirt and Tony's black trousers. What they were saying and doing existed somewhere above my head in another world, until I caught sight of the revolver in Tony's hand. Then, I quickly scrambled to my feet and clung to Mama's mourning skirt which she always wore in honor of a distantly miscarried baby.

"I tell you, he cannot stay here," Mama said.

"Shut up," her eldest son snarled.

"You will end up in jail, or you will be killed, Antonio." Mama was breathing hard, and I had the feeling that if Tony wasn't careful, she might take the stove poker to him.

Tony twirled the barrel of his gun which was aimed under the sink, and checked to see that all chambers were loaded.

"The man must go, and that's that." Mama attempted to finalize the matter.

"Shut up!" Tony commanded again and made a couple of stabs

12

with his gun into the electrified air.

Because he truly was the boss, Mama said no more and Tony slipped the gun into his hip pocket.

"He'll stay here in my room until I tell you it is time for him to leave. You will take him three meals a day, but no one will see him or speak to him. Here is the money for the first week's food, " Tony finished defiantly, slamming a few bills and a handful of change onto the blue-checked oilcloth of the kitchen table.

Tony went back to his room and the unseen visitor, banging the door shut behind him. Mama, defeated and mad, grabbed me by the shoulders and angrily admonished me not to follow in my brother's footsteps. When she moved away to the sink, I slipped a penny off the table into my pocket and flew down the stairs to join the Niccoli boys.

Francesco and Thomaso were waiting for me because we had agreed the day before to watch the funeral together. It was a fine day, the sun shining down between the tenement buildings, a sense of solemnity in the air. The vestibule of Tommy's apartment house had been filled with wreaths and bouquets sent by family members and friends the day before. From our stoop across the street we especially admired the black funerary drapings around the entry and the bright flower spray on the door.

"I saw them put it up yesterday," Francesco bragged in Italian. (We usually spoke Italian; we knew very little English.)

"I saw it, too. It was the undertaker who did it," Thomaso chimed in, proudly exhibiting his superior knowledge.

"Well, *I* saw Frankie Yale go up to Chevi's last night," Francesco said, continuing the game of one-upmanship. "He's the biggest gangster in the world."

But it was I, four-year-old Giovanni Torccio, who had the best news of all, announcing loftily, "You know what I got? I got a penny!" Pulling the penny out of my pocket, I told them that I was buying a treat for the three of us.

On the way to the candy store, Francesco said, "Let's buy nigger babies. I like them most."

"*E mio soldo.*" It was my penny, and I would buy with it what I wanted.

Once inside the store, we eagerly surveyed the possibilities: Indian nuts, corn candy, Tootsie rolls, two kinds of licorice whips, jelly beans, chocolate kisses, cinnamon-flavored sugar-coated peanuts, and chocolate-covered goobers. Since it was my penny, we

13

agreed that I would do all of the talking as we proceeded with our usual number on old man Moskowitz, the Italian-Jew who owned the store.

"How much is this, *Signoro*?" I asked drawing his attention to a tray of nigger babies on the bottom shelf in the corner.

He told me, and then I was attracted to the dark brown and naturally sweet bean-pods laid out on a counter tray.

"Could I buy three of these with my penny, *Signoro*? Then all of us could have some." I pleaded with my eyes as well as my words.

As I continued to distract the old man, *mio compagni* stuffed their pockets with anything they could lay their hands on. In the end I bought according to volume, as usual, getting roasted *ce ce* peas that the storekeeper measured from a small wooden cup into my hands. We staked out our seats on the curb across from the Chevi apartment early, and shared the peas and pilfered sweets. We were close friends and stuck together. It was a lesson we had already learned.

Mourners were gathering across the street, and soon six Navy men in full-dress uniform went into the apartment. A few minutes later they emerged with the flag-draped casket and slid it into the hearse that had just arrived.

"It's de 'dead-wagon'," Thomaso said, lapsing from Italian into English.

"It ain't a 'dead-wagon.' It's a hoise. My brudder talks American, and he says it's a hoise," Francesco replied.

This vehicle in which Tommy Chevi was to take his last ride was truly a fine wagon: glass windows and doors draped with black curtains trimmed in white tassels; a black shiny frame; and on the very top a "catlick" cross. The driver sat up front in charge of the great black horse whose harness was decorated with ivory rings and brass knobs. Even the horse's hooves were ready for the occasion, having been blackened and painted with used motor oil.

The hired band arrived en masse and took their position in front of the hearse. When the first notes of the dirge sounded, we knew the long-awaited moment had come, stood at attention and made the sign of the cross.

"*Nome di Padre, Figlio, e Spirito Santo. Amen,*" we said in unison as the procession began.

Off went the band and hearse up 65th Street and around the corner, circling the block before heading down toward Saint Rosalie's Church. They would pass by our reviewing position twice. Behind the hearse came the immediate family and closest friends, weeping

14

and moaning, lurching and staggering under the weight of their grief. The more composed mourners supported the distraught as best they could. Neighbors and passers-by stood on the sidewalk, doffed their hats and silently crossed themselves if they were Catholic.

Then the "flower-cars" got underway and our excitement escalated. Now we had to be especially alert and vigilant so as not to miscount. In the front seat beside each driver were the sprays and wreaths while the very largest floral piece was arranged carefully in the back against the folded top of the touring car. The fragrant and colorful onslaught was the closest thing to a flower garden that we had ever seen.

"Look at dem cahnations," I said. All flowers were carnations as far as we were concerned.

Francesco was the only one of us who could count, so it was up to him now.

"Der dey come," shouted Thomaso.

"Der's number one," shouted Francesco.

As each car passed, I slipped a pea into my shirt pocket just in case, somewhere along the line, Francesco lost track. When the last car had passed, the band was already around the block and turning up 65th Street again. Francesco had counted twenty-seven flower-cars, and the peas in my pocket matched his total. Twenty-seven flower-cars! The most we had ever heard of!

When I went home, Mama saw a couple of peas in my pocket and somehow got it out of me that I had stolen a penny. She gave me a good whipping and warned me that I would grow up to be just like Tony if I didn't stop it.

That night before we ate supper, Mama sent Angelina to Tony's room with a plate of food for our unseen guest. Angelina knocked on the door and when it opened, a hand reached out and took the food.

At the table I told of the procession and the twenty-seven cars as Papa drank from the wine flask and passed it around to us kids. Mama frowned a lot, a frown I was to see on her face quite often during the month that the stranger remained hidden in Tony's room.

One morning I realized that no one had taken a breakfast plate to our unwanted guest, and I overheard Mama asking Tony who he was and where he had gone.

"Shut up and don't ask questions," he growled, letting all of us know that it was none of our business.

The guest to whom we could not speak had slipped away in the night as mysteriously as he had come on the day of Tommy's funeral.

A Sunday Dinner and a Shooting

Weekends were special. Every Saturday morning I got to go on the ice route with Papa. We didn't have a clock so we never knew exactly what time it was, and I can only surmise that Papa must have wakened automatically in the mornings. We always left very early and without breakfast. In spite of the fact I was hungry, I didn't think much about it because Papa seldom ate but one meal a day.

I enjoyed going with Papa, and even though he never showed any of us younger children much tenderness, he never beat us either because Mama would not let him. She personally administered all of our beatings, and they were regular and no-nonsense.

Papa was a rather short man—about five-foot-six—thin and wiry. He seldom smiled, perhaps because life in America had not turned out to be the dream of good times he expected. And, though life in Italy had been difficult, at least it had been lived among friends in the quiet of the countryside, amid the fragrance of the basil fields. Here in Brooklyn, Papa worked as hard as he had in the old country, but, in addition, he had to put up with the noise and strange new ways of a teeming city. To make matters worse, he could not speak English and was competing with thousands of other immigrants who could. No wonder his face was lined, and his hair prematurely gray.

His most memorable features were his eyes—one was gray and the other was blue. This difference in color made him appear somewhat uncertain or vague, as though through the blue eye he saw the world in one way and through the gray, another. Otherwise, Papa looked like the rest of the immigrant ice peddlers with their baggy black pants that ended two or three inches above the tops of their heavy shoes and their burlap capes. The men made these hooded capes from feed sacks, the burlap anchoring the ice on their shoulders and giving them thin protection against the cold.

On our way to the stable, I followed closely behind Papa, imitating the way he walked with his toes pointed out almost ninety degrees from his heels. I forced myself to stretch my toes in that way at a time when my bones were forming, and after several years of this ridiculous mimicking, I still find myself walking more like a duck than a human.

Though we had gone without breakfast, Papa was careful to feed Jim, the horse, generously. Then, as Papa curried and harnessed him, I darted back and forth underneath the belly of the good-natured animal, testing my courage and developing my agility.

And though Papa wore only his burlap sack for protection, Jim had a black rubberized raincoat for rainy days and a handsome fringed net for hot days when the flies were bad. During the snows of winter, Jim had other special equipment—leather covers that fit over the tops of his hooves and held three delicate but strong chains across the underside of his feet so he would not slip.

After helping Papa load the wagon with blocks of ice, I rode up front sitting proudly beside him on the high seat. Most of his customers were in the Borough Park District, which was just three blocks away in distance, but miles away in wealth. These people lived in two-story row-houses and could afford to spend fifteen or twenty cents a day just for ice.

All morning Papa cut the heavy blocks of ice and carried the pieces with tongs, holding them against the burlap that protected his shoulder. Up the steps he went, disappearing into the houses where he deposited his load into the ice boxes and collected the pennies that supported our family.

When noontime came, we stopped to feed Jim, but there was no lunch for us. Instead, Papa lit up his short piece of Italian cigar, and I refreshed myself with bits of shaved ice.

At the end of the day, we went by Peter Bollo's feed store to pick up the hay and oats that Jim needed for the coming week. I was always fascinated by the old Jewish couple who lived in a small room just inside the door of the feed store. Their living quarters, partitioned off from the rest of the cavernous building, contained a two-burner gas stove, a table with two chairs, and a cot on which only one of them could possibly have slept. They earned their living by mending burlap sacks for a penny apiece. The man wore his traditional black yarmulka and the woman her black shawl as they worked swiftly, reweaving the old sacks that had been torn or chewed by rats.

On this particular Saturday Papa stayed longer than usual talking with Mr. Bollo, whose soldier son had been killed while fighting in France.

Grieving, the father said, "My Leonardo should be home any day now. The government said they would send him home to me soon,"

Papa put a comforting hand on his shoulder. "I hear there is a boat in the harbor today. Surely your Leonardo is on it."

Papa bought a live rooster at the chicken market on our way home and presented it to Mama, who knew exactly what to do. She deftly folded the bird's neck back over her index finger and cut the jugular vein open with a sharp knife. Then she held the chicken over a skillet and drained the blood out to make a special Saturday night treat. Seasoned with a little salt, the blood was heated slowly until it clotted into a cake which Mama divided among us. We were starved, and the small squares of fried blood tasted very good.

We stood around watching Mama as she continued preparations for Sunday dinner. After the chicken had been plucked and the insides removed, she took out the intestines, split them with a scissors, washed them well, and cut them into small pieces which, along with the liver, gizzard and heart were made into broth. The chicken feet were boiled and scaled, the head was plucked and cleaned and then these, too, were added to the pot.

In the morning Papa took Mike and Angie to Saint Rosalie's Church, where he earned a little money cleaning up after mass. I stayed back with Mama as she continued to prepare for our weekly feast. She rolled pasta dough into long pale ropes which were then cut into half-inch pieces. Working quickly and silently, because life was serious and without time for idle talk or play with children, she drew her fingertip deftly through the dough which then fashioned itself almost magically into *orecchiotelli* (little ears) or *scamaruchelle* (seashells) as I watched in amazement.

By the time Papa and the kids were back from church, the flat was filled with the delicious smells of the simmering sauce that Mama had made from *conserva di pomidoro* (tomato puree). This had been cooked, strained, then cooked down again until it was a thick paste which then had been preserved in jars with leaves of basil and olive oil on top. Now, it simmered away slowly with onion, garlic and other herbs, tempting us almost beyond our ability to endure until dinner time.

And then it was time for me to go to the corner saloon and call Tony. I was happy to go, not only because it meant we would eat soon, but because every time I went there, Tony would tell the bartender to give me something to drink. Usually Gimpy, the bartender who had been wounded in the war, gave me a glass of water with a few drops of anisette in it.

"The kid's here," Gimpy called to Tony as he saw me hanging around the door. I would not enter until I had been spoken to.

18

"Give him the usual," Tony ordered as I walked in.

While Gimpy prepared my drink, my eyes adjusted to the darkness of the saloon, and I saw a group of men around a table playing cards. Each player had either a gun or a knife beside his cash pile, and everything was very serious with no joking around. Irish and Slug, two good friends who were constantly together around the neighborhood, sat across from each other.

Even though it was prohibition, the men were drinking openly, and even though gambling was illegal they were deeply involved in their cards regardless of the fact that the door was open.

"Mama wants you to come home and eat," I said to Tony

"Ok, kid. I'll be right there."

I drank my anisette water and went home. When Tony arrived, everyone sat down to dinner but Mama. The Italian housewife always fed her husband first, her kids next, and herself last. Papa started dinner by taking a drink of homemade Dago red from the flask before passing it on to us kids. We were all expected to take at least one drink so our blood would be strong and we would sleep well. It took more than a little mastering to be able to drink from the cherry-wood flask that looked like a small barrel with a vent hole and a spout. You had to plug the hole with your finger as you lifted the flask above your head, then unplug at the right time so the wine would stream out the spout into your open mouth. Papa was very good at doing this and held the flask up high so that the wine trickled directly down into his swallowing gullet.

As the wine was going around, Mama served the soup. Papa was first and he got the head of the rooster which he opened with his fingers and held toward me offering the brains. I picked those out and ate the sweet treat with relish. Tony and the other little kids each got a special part in their soup, too: a foot, a heart or a gizzard. We each had our own plate and ate from no other. Mine was a small oval dish, and when Mama put it in front of me, there were bits of dandelion and intestine floating in the broth. A grater and chunk of hard Parmesan were then sent around, and we each waited impatiently to put a sprinkling of cheese into our soup.

The pasta came to the table on a large oval platter. Papa served himself and us little kids, and whatever was put on our plates, we ate. Bread was passed and everyone was expected to break a piece off and fill up on it so there would be enough pasta to go around. Sometimes we didn't want any bread, but we took it anyway so Papa would not single us out with the hated accusation, "What's the matter? Is the

19

bread made of flour?"

Then came the chicken that had been roasted with potatoes and herbs served with a salad of escarole and dandelions. Finally, dessert arrived. This was always Italian bread dipped in wine, and it was something that I found I could pass. But I stayed in my seat because soon Mama would bring out homemade *prosciutto*, *salami*, and sausage. And sometimes there would be nuts and fruit.

Papa and Tony remained at the table to smoke and drink, continuing the dinner conversation that had been mostly of the *mano nera* (the Black Hand). As the afternoon wore on, they got hungry again and began the eating that might continue for hours. Just before I left the room to go outside and play, I heard Papa say, "Peter Bollo expects Leonardo's body home from the war any day now. He was very sad yesterday when Giovanni and I were there."

"When the body arrives, it won't be his son anyway. There's no knowing whose son will be in that pine box," Tony replied.

Out on the stoop the Niccoli boys and I watched the people walk by. Suddenly, we heard yelling from the saloon down the street and then shots. Shootings were not all that unusual; we had seen them before, but they still scared us. Before we could leave, Irish and Slug staggered out of the saloon, both wounded. Slug leaned against the doorway, slipped down in slow motion and was dead by the time he reached the sidewalk. Irish lurched across the street toward the police booth on the corner. The cop on duty made a hasty retreat on his bicycle, so he wouldn't learn too much and have to go to court to testify. Irish had killed his best friend. The police never got into the argument, and that ended it.

Water in the Gutter Under Clear Skies
and Kerosene and Citrate of Magnesia on Saturday Night

Looking back, those early days were pretty grim: lots of death and dying. At the time, of course, I was quite happy because I figured that was the way life was supposed to be. A funeral procession can be as exciting as a circus parade; a street shooting as stimulating as a ghost story before bed. Since Mama and Papa were so busy with mere survival, there was no time to play with us or tell us stories—even if they had been so inclined. Today, when I am asked to teach a class of children a story or song from my childhood, I simply have none because they were not part of my growing up. Nevertheless, since it is the nature of children to be bright and full of expectation, many

20

of our joyous occasions grew simply out of the everyday and mundane.

One of these occasions was Monday morning—washday. I watched and stayed out from underfoot as Mama wrapped the dirty laundry in a sheet and carried it down the steps. Then, off we went together along the street, Mama balancing the laundry perfectly on her head. She was small but strong from hard work in the fields in Italy and the never-ending job of raising a big family. As far as I can recall, she had two dresses—both black—one for washing and one for wearing. Mama wore her graying black hair puffed out in pompadour around her face and wound into a braided bun in back. Her face was pretty and her blue eyes were quick as a bird's—always alert.

I carried the big bar of Octagon soap. Probably the soap wasn't as big as I remember it because I was so little, but it seems that the tan bar weighed at least two pounds. I was one proud kid to be helping Mama, no matter what it took.

Octagon soap was used for everything, not just the laundry. We washed dishes with it and our faces. We took baths with Octagon soap, and used it for shampoos as well as scrubbing the floor. To this day I can recall the strong antiseptic smell—more potent than the early Lifebuoy bars.

On this particular Monday morning, I not only carried the Octagon soap, but I had the washboard as well. It was not easy handling both of these items, but I managed to get them to the basement of the tenement building where Mama would do the laundry. All of the neighborhood Italian women came here to wash their clothes and catch up on the latest news from the old country.

When the wash was finished, Mama bundled the wet laundry in a sheet, and we started home. Soon, we met Signora Matti and Signora Grecco, and stopped to talk. Angelo Grecco and I were about the same age and became preoccupied with our own conversation about starting school as the women discussed the pressure being put upon their husbands to join the Street Peddlers Protective Association.

The three women, wearing their ever-present long black dresses with black shawls because they were always mourning someone, carried bulky bundles of laundry comfortably on their heads. Angelo and I were balancing on the edge of the curb when I noticed water trickling down the gutter.

"Look, Angelo." I pointed to the small stream and then looked

21

up to check the sky for rain. But the sky was clear.

"Where does the water come from?" I asked Angelo.

As the stream continued, we became more and more animated. Water welling up like a miracle out of the gutter dust! At last, I could bear it no longer, and pulled on Mama's skirt to get her attention. I got her attention all right, and Mama got my ear between her thumb and forefinger and jerked me around by this rather tender appendage commanding, *"Silenzio."* I still didn't know what was happening, but I got the rather painful message that I had better stop noticing the water in the gutter. It was then I realized the source of the mystery fluid. Senora Matti, standing close to the curb edge, her skirt pinched out rather elegantly at the crotch, her legs spread, was peeing perfectly into the gutter, certainly without missing a word being said and, probably without wetting herself with so much as a drop.

The Monday morning laundry schedule was a pleasant outing for the most part, but the Saturday night ritual that took place in our kitchen before bedtime was anything but pleasant. Angelina, Michael and I were regularly shampooed and purged as Mama attempted to keep us lice-free and healthy. We never did get lice like most of the other kids, so Mama's prescription worked, but lice might have been preferable to what we went through to avoid them.

Mike was the oldest of us three young ones, so he was first. By the time I watched Mama dunk his and Angelina's heads in kerosene, and shampoo their hair with Octagon soap, I knew the agony that was coming to me next.

The dreaded basin of kerosene was placed on a chair, and Mama grabbed me none-too-gently by the scruff of the neck and immersed my hair in it. She probably only rubbed and scrubbed for a few minutes, but it seemed like an hour. No matter how hard I closed my eyes, I always got kerosene and Octagon soap in them, so during the rest of the evening, I alternately rubbed my burning eyes and bawled. But Mama was not deterred from her mission of cleaning us thoroughly, both inside and out, before bed on Saturday night. When she was convinced no louse inhabited my hair, she went after my skin with a washrag and Octagon soap. My misery spared me nothing as Mama polished my face to a high luster before proceeding. She worked downwards, methodically scouring and scrubbing every inch, every fold of my naked body until I shone like one of the angels in a church picture. And, then, Mama stood back to admire her work. It did not matter that my eyes were red and swollen, that my skin had been all but worn away; it only mattered that I was clean and without vermin.

But Mama was not finished yet. Oh, no! Now came the worst part; the inner cleansing. When Mama gave the first cupful of citrate of magnesia to Michael, the bilious green walls of the kitchen began closing in on me, and by the time Angelina had been given her purgative, I was already beginning to gag in anticipation. But neither gagging nor bawling was to deter Mama from her determined cleansings.

The hated and bitter cup was pressed to my lips and Mama's hand went up and down before my face indicating that there was no other possibility but to drink. The magnesia slipped into my gullet and always came back again to my mouth before finally reaching my stomach. The laxative never stayed there very long, either, as uncontrollable vomiting brought it back to the wash basin. I suppose to Mama it did not matter that the medicine was regurgitated just as long as it had been in the stomach for even a brief time.

Shortly thereafter, it was time for the customary goodnight kiss. This was normally a pleasant experience, but on Saturday night there was very little affection on my part.

A Pack of Troubles

My older brother, Pasquali or Pat as we came to call him, was about seventeen when he went to work washing dishes and learning to become a cook in a restaurant. This job introduced him to tomato ketchup and white American bread. In our household we had never seen either because we ate only Italian-style food. The bread that Pat brought home was tried and rejected because it tasted like cotton compared to the substantial hard-crust Italian bread. The ketchup also was unacceptable because we were not accustomed to the sweetness. So Pat's early attempts to Americanize our palates fell flat.

Sometime during the early months of 1922, tragedy struck when Pat came home and announced that he had been diagnosed as having tuberculosis. Mama put Pat to bed in the room at the end of the flat as far away from the family as possible and none of us kids saw him in that room ever. Mama took him his food and, as far as the rest of the family was concerned, Pat was a non-person from then on, a vague coughing presence who existed on the periphery of our lives.

More trouble came to us that year when Graziano, now known

as Harry, came home unexpectedly from his residential Catholic high school wearing a soldier's uniform. Mama and Papa, like many Italian parents, dreamed of having one son become a priest, and Harry had been their great hope. Father Locksley Appo had assured our family that Harry would make a good priest, but he had not foreseen Harry's direction or *misdirection* as it turned out.

Harry took up with a married woman and left via the bedroom window one night when her husband came home unexpectedly. At this time Harry figured he had better get as far away as possible, and the army offered him an assignment in Hawaii. There went the hopes of Mama and Papa and Father Appo. Harry stayed home for about an hour telling of his dilemma, and after that night he never saw our parents again. We lost track of him entirely, and by the time he looked me up years later, Mama and Papa were both dead.

About that time Tony brought another surprise home to us. Appearing unexpectedly with a Jewish girl on his arm, he announced, "This is Bessie, my new wife." Just what we needed: a sister-in-law who couldn't speak Italian. Bessie joined Tony in the room where he had kept the mysterious stranger hidden, and it was here that the first grandchild was born.

Tony was not present at the birth because he was becoming more and more involved with the underworld. I don't know where Papa was, but I do remember Mike, Angie and I were in our bedroom, wide-eyed and a little scared at the presence of a midwife. At the height of all the commotion, we heard Mama announce with considerable gusto, *"E una piccola ragazza."*

Since she didn't understand Italian, we probably knew before Bessie that she had given birth to a girl. Little Rosalie was a fine baby, but her presence was one more factor to add to the already crowded apartment. About a week after she was born, Mama put a needle and thread through the baby's ear so she could wear earrings. When Rosie was sick from time to time, Mama's remedies for her included lots of prayer and folk cures such as garlic poultices and hot applications which were placed upon the poor baby's bare belly.

Something good happened to me in the midst of these family problems. Bessie took me to the Board of Health for a smallpox vaccination so I could be enrolled in kindergarten. It was a great relief to have someone speak for me in English, and I was pretty excited about my new adventure in spite of the fact that it was beginning with this none too-pleasant medical procedure. Hardened as I was by slaps and whacks, by kerosene and citrate of magnesia, by falls and scrapes that were not healed with kisses but with beatings, I took the puncturing of my arm with equanimity. As the doctor pricked away, he asked Bessie, "Is this little man your son?"

"No," she replied. "He is my brother-in-law." I felt proud at being spoken about in English.

Outside the kindergarten classroom there was the usual playground hubbub, but these calls and shouts were almost all in various foreign languages. We called the kids who spoke English "Protestants" because we knew only three kinds of people: Jews, Catholics, and Protestants. Inside the classroom, English was the only language, of course, and I began adding to the few words I had learned from Mike, Angie and Bessie.

As I was launched in kindergarten and things got better for me, life became more difficult for Pat. A Board of Health doctor sent him to a local hospital because his condition was deteriorating. One day Father Appo came for all of our family and took us in his chauffeur-driven car to see Pat in a dismal ward with thirty or forty other tubercular patients. Not long after that, Father arranged for Pat to be admitted to a TB sanatorium in Suffern, New York.

By now Mama was very depressed and not feeling well. Her teeth were giving her a lot of trouble and I began hearing Mama had something called "diabetes." All these troubles probably reinforced her natural tendency to want me strong enough to survive in the hostile environment of the world I was to grow up in. When I fell down, I got whipped for falling, when I bawled, I got slapped for bawling. The day I fell off Papa's ice wagon and split my head open, she poured wine vinegar into the wash basin and kept dunking my open wound into the acetic antiseptic. Mama believed that any medicine that hurt was doing good. We could not afford iodine or peroxide, so she used the vinegar she had in the cupboard. She would not have used Mercurochrome if we had it because, although it was red and this was a good sign, it did not hurt when applied to open wounds. When she felt certain the vinegar had done its work, she wrapped a rag around my head, gave me a couple of whacks for being clumsy and sat me in the chair to think about it. I didn't mind too much because I expected it. One thing about Mama, she was consistent.

It was just one thing after another: a son in the TB sanatorium; another intended for the priesthood who had to drop out of school because he got involved with a married woman; and a third son tangled up with the underworld. And to make matters worse Papa's income was shrinking as he had to pay the Street Peddlers Protective

Association more and more of his meagre earnings. Mama decided to do something drastic.

Mama Arranges An Exorcism

Mama and two of her friends were sitting around the kitchen table as I came in from school. The jar of leeches that was kept on the shelf along with Mama's home-canned tomatoes sat empty on the table before them. The women had opened the fronts of their dresses that were all made large and blousy for matters of nursing and carrying packages, and sat contentedly with two or three leeches sucking on each full white bosom. I often saw this scene, because the women believed these sucking creatures were a deterrent against high blood pressure and helped to rid the body of other blood-carried poisons. Soon, they removed the leeches and put them back into the jar and returned their pale melon breasts to their proper places.

"Someone has put the *malocchio* (evil eye) on our family," I heard Mama telling one of her friends. "Not only my three oldest sons are in trouble, but now we have two more mouths to feed just when my husband's salary becomes less each week. And my health is not good. I am so tired all of the time, and, lately, my teeth hurt. See, it pains all of the time." She opened her mouth so her friend could look deep inside past the two gold crowns she wore proudly over her eyeteeth.

Senora Grecco made sucking sounds of commiseration with her tongue as she noted the abscesses. "Tich, tich," she said, moving her head sadly from side to side, "but who could have put the evil eye on you?"

"I do not know, but I cannot go on like this. Bad luck comes again and again to this household. And I grow more and more tired each day. You mentioned that your cousin who just arrived from Italy wears the golden horn and knows about these matters," Mama said wearily.

And so an exorcism was arranged. A day was chosen, and a fee of two dollars was agreed upon. In a matter of days the newcomer to America appeared at our door with her cousin Senora Grecco. The proceedings were carried out in the kitchen around the table. Mike, Angie and I were sent to our bedroom next to the kitchen, but with the door cracked, we could see the three women working under the dim gas light that hung from the ceiling.

Mama wore a gold cross around her neck; Senora Grecco and her cousin wore gold animal horns. They were all dressed in black, but, of course, this was not unusual as they were always dressed in black. Mama and Senora Grecco shrank back in fear as they watched the exorcist pull a large black cross out of her dress and hold it before her. The woman began a low chanting that was probably calculated to repel any evil spirits in the neighborhood and walked around the kitchen swinging the cross in front of her. She stopped at every corner of the room, where she spoke her most fierce warnings, touching the cross now to her heart, now to her forehead and completing each ritual with a kiss of the cross. When she began a counterclockwise march and chant around the table where Mama and Senora Grecco sat, the sheer terror was too much for Mama, and she cried out as she dropped her head to the table.

The exorcism must have been a folk-mixture of pagan and Christian rituals. And that would be fine with Mama who could not read or write in any language. And though she attended mass she could not understand the Latin, so her religious understanding probably did not extend far beyond the sign of the cross. We three little kids fell asleep before the evening was over, but in the morning Mama seemed to be in better spirits than usual.

"Life will be easier now that the evil eye is removed from us," she said.

More Trouble—A Robbery

Three days later black handprints appeared mysteriously on the gymnasium wall of my school. The *mano nera!* We kids were scared and I did not dally on my way home that afternoon. The black hand was something to be reckoned with. I had heard that in Italy the *brigante* kidnapped poor little boys and sold them into servitude in rich families. Sometimes they took young girls and sold them to rich widowers or older men to be trained as mistresses.

Home and Mama would be a welcome refuge that day as I ran scared up 65th Street, not even slowing down to glance into the candy store window.

"Mama," I burst into the kitchen, "the *mano nera* was at school..." my voice trailed off when I saw the sight at the kitchen table. There sat Mama and two of her friends holding their heads and weeping.

Their story came out in sobs and moans and great sweeping gestures that seemed to ask, "How can this be?" The three women had been working rather happily shelling peas in our kitchen when two robbers burst in. One held a gun on them while the other took the plain gold wedding bands from their fingers. Oh, the misery of

27

losing your most valued possession, the symbol of marriage which meant you were fulfilling your purpose on earth! And beyond that, the robbers had extracted thirty cents from Mama—every cent she had left in the house for food until Papa's next ice delivery.

"The *malocchio*, the *malocchio*," Mama moaned. "*No e finito.*"

My story about the black handprints on the gymnasium wall paled to nothing in comparison to what had happened at the flat. The women did not attempt to go to the police booth on the corner. What good would it do? They could not explain in English what had happened, and besides, what could the police do? What *would* the police do? So Mama and her friends continued their grieving until it was time to begin supper for their families

Mama Dies

Mama was sick and getting sicker. Perhaps the return of the evil eye was too much for her; perhaps it speeded up her illness by throwing her into depression. Sick as she was, however, she did not go to bed. And Papa continued to fulfill his part of the marriage bargain, to bring home the money. Angie helped Mama the best she could, and Mike and I spent a lot of time out on the stoop. Then one day when Papa had gone to feed the horse, Mama lay down and went into a deep sleep. Bessie summoned a doctor, but Mama was dead by the time he got to our house.

When Papa got home, Bessie sent Mike to get Father Appo who went straight to Mama's room and prayed in Latin. We three little kids were huddled together on the bed in the room next to Mama's when he came in to comfort us. I can still see that straight handsome figure, so tall his black curly hair nearly touched the top of the doorway. He stood there for a moment looking at us sadly with large brown eyes, and it is only in retrospect that the perfect Italian with which he began to comfort us seems surprising. The kindness that he showed to us was innate and not something that he had learned, however. It was beyond the boundaries of language or countries.

We jumped to our feet and kissed Father's hand as we had been taught, and then he did something most unusual for us. He put his arms around us and and drew us to him. This was the only real comfort we were to receive when our mother died. I don't remember the words that Father used to comfort us, but I still remember the tenderness and affection with which he spoke them. He spoke softly and slowly, every word gentle as a whisper.

28

After Father left, another man came: a stranger. Mike, Angie, and I were still huddled on the bed as he walked through our room to Mama's carrying a bag and other equipment. We had heard Papa say the embalmer was coming, but I, at least, did not understand. When the stranger appeared at our door and inquired, "Where's the toilet?" Angie pulled me to her, turning my eyes away.

"Don't look, Giovanni!" she cried.

But it was already too late. I had seen the two large jars of blood that he was carrying. For years afterward, I thought our mother had bled to death.

Mama's funeral was not as grand as Tommy Chevi's. Oh, there were maroon drapings in the living room where Mama was laid out on a bier. There were black drapings around our apartment entrance and a wreath on the door. But Papa could not afford to hire a band, and when Mama was put into a coffin and carried down the stairs there were not many people waiting below. When the fine hearse came and started off down the street, I did not follow with the others. I sat down on the curb with the Niccoli boys and watched the cortege disappear around the corner on its way to Saint Rosalie's.

There was one flower-car.

About a week later Tony appeared at the door with two large vegetable baskets and began breaking our dishes into them. Papa was beside himself.

"What are you doing? Have you lost your mind?" he shouted.

"The *malocchio* is on us, and the only way to get rid of it is to destroy everything of Mama's," Tony replied.

So, over Papa's protests, he continued smashing all of the dishes into the basket. Everything went: even my treasured white oval plate. And just to be sure, Tony finished by crashing Pat's bottle of ketchup into Mama's broken dishes.

The red sauce that ran thickly among the shards reminded me of the embalmer in our room the morning that Mama died.

2

The Family Breaks Up

An Orphanage Looms

Papa stood dejected and downcast, listening to Tony.

"This place has *il malocchio*, and we're leaving," Tony said. "You better get out of here, too. Besides, you can't afford this big flat. You need to find a smaller place."

Papa didn't say a word. It wouldn't have done any good if he had because Tony was the boss.

"The kids are too much for you to take care of. Mike can go live with Father McCarthy, and you can put Angie and Johnny in a home," Tony continued.

Still Papa said nothing as we three little kids hovered anxiously in the room, our fate seemingly being decided by our oldest brother. A home! The words struck terror to my six-year-old heart. "A home" meant an orphanage, and I had seen the tall brick walls topped with shards of glass where the orphans lived under the watchful eye of the nuns.

A few days later Papa enlisted the aid of a *'paesano* and moved us the three blocks to 62nd Street. They loaded his ice wagon with little more than the bare necessities: a table and four chairs; a small marble-top dresser; and two beds (one of which we three kids would share, with me sleeping in the middle, my head toward the foot). The luxuries included the Victrola, a picture of Christ with his bleeding heart on the outside of his robe, and a glass holding a candle that was always kept lighted in honor of Mama. Papa hand-carried his beloved records of Enrico Caruso and Amelita Galli-Curci which he played on Sundays after our noon meal. When the voice of Caruso filled our new flat, I remembered the fight between Mama and Papa after he first brought the records home. Mama felt they could not afford them, but Papa loved opera very much especially when sung by an Italian.

An Orphanage Looms

Our new ground-floor flat was just down the block from the hated orphanage. I knew what that meant. Papa was getting Angie and me used to the idea of being put into a home, so I hung around outside as much as I could learning what was in store for me. It was even worse than I imagined. The orphans were not allowed to come to the fence to talk to us street kids when we called to them, and they had to attend mass all the time. They were prisoners as far as I was concerned, jailed behind ugly walls impossible to scale.

Once a week, weather permitting, the nuns would lead them in silence around the block, and that was their only outing. The children, ranging in age from four to twelve, were disciplined to the point they would not speak to each other on these walks. I would rather have died than be put into such a place and live like that. Life on the street had its drawbacks, but it was preferable to prison, I knew that. I also knew that if orphans were not adopted by the time they were twelve, they became priests or nuns and never got out from behind those fortress-like walls.

If it had not been for the fact that Father Appo's parish house was directly across the street from our new apartment, despair over the orphanage looming in my future might have really overwhelmed me. But when things got too scary, just seeing Father gave me a certain comfort.

Father Appo raised Great Danes in a small cage behind his house. The dogs had puppies that summer, and though the smell was often horrendous, the little animals responded to my attention with wet tongues and soft paws. Just inside the back door was the machine Father's assistant used for stamping Eucharist wafers from thin sheets of bread. I had eaten the wafer scraps before on visits with Papa, but never had they been as welcome as that summer, because there was less food to eat at home now. Talking with the priests kept me from thinking too much about the orphanage, and Father Appo allowed me to play with the great box of pennies. These I stacked into skyscrapers of money that occupied my attention and protected me from my loneliness for Mama and the Niccoli boys, and my fear of *the home.* Eventually though, the pennies would tumble helter-skelter to the wooden floor and my sadness would crash in upon me again.

Sex Education alla Geraldo

As the days went by, and Papa did not send me off to the orphanage, I began to feel a little better and even started to mingle with some of the 62nd Street kids. Maybe, just maybe, Papa would be able to keep us together, and maybe this new neighborhood wouldn't be so bad after all. Most of the kids were older, but I hung around on the edges of the crowd and was beginning to know some names. These street kids gave me my first lesson in reproduction that summer.

Geraldo swaggered up to me smoking a butt he had found in the gutter and demanded, "Do you know where you come from, kid?"

"What do you mean?" I replied. Geraldo knew as well as I that we had come from 65th Street.

"How you wuz born."

I was very nervous being noticed by Geraldo, but I felt relieved to be able to answer his question because Mama had informed me about this matter. "Yeah," I said. "I was born from dust in a corner."

Geraldo indicated his complete contempt by spitting on the sidewalk. "Ah shit—You wuz born from your mudder's twat."

Having given an answer unacceptable to him, I was too embarrassed and confused to reply at first, but as the horrible Geraldo hovered over me, I finally managed, "What's a *twat*?"

"That's how ladies piss," he explained loftily.

Well, now, the body part that pisses, that was something I could relate to, but the rest was very confusing. I stood there speechless and bewildered, trying to picture how a baby could come out of this part of a grown-up body. As Geraldo continued berating me as a "dumb shit," I saw something that he did not see: a young parish priest had come up behind him, and in those days, priests disciplined street kids whenever and wherever they deemed it necessary. Father Joseph grabbed Geraldo by the neck, gave him a good shaking and then a swift kick in the ass, surprising him so much that he almost swallowed the cigarette butt. This definitely got Geraldo's attention for the dressing-down he was about to receive. The rest of us kids were delighted, but we did not dare show our pleasure for Geraldo would be around long after the priest had gone. And, of course, Geraldo did not dare tell his parents he had been manhandled by a priest. The church was the law in those matters, and relating the story would only have resulted in another kick in the ass.

I Find Forty Dollars and Receive a Little Lord Fauntleroy Suit

Father Appo was transferred a couple of months after we moved to 62nd Street, and perhaps that is why Papa decided to move, too. We went to a smaller apartment on 61st Street; I took it as a good sign that Papa might not put us in the orphanage after all.

Papa did the best he could to keep us clean and fed, I suppose, but it was tough because the Street Peddlers Protective Society was demanding more and more of his meagre income. I had one outfit of clothes, and, on the rare occasions when Papa washed them, I sat around in my pants while my BVDs, shirt, and socks dried on the line. Actually, Papa and I both sat around in our pants because he washed his shirt and union suit at the same time, but never our trousers. Mike and Angie had to look out for themselves.

Papa didn't bother about having us bathe or anything like that. When we washed our faces and hands, we simply scrubbed a little of the dirt away under the faucet in the kitchen sink and dried off on the heavy cement sack that was our only towel. Toward the end of summer, however, Papa decided to do something about our hair because we would soon start a new school in our new neighborhood. Angie's got a scrubbing with Octagon soap, and it looked considerably better. Mike and I, however, were not to fare so well. We were too poor to afford haircuts, so Papa had our heads shaved. We were humiliated. We had become baldies and the subject for taunts and jeers by the kids who could afford haircuts.

Brother Mike had never paid too much attention to me before Mama died, and I will never know if his concern now was out of sympathy or embarrassment, but he made me a skullcap that summer. Mike had a skullcap of his own that partially hid the shame of his shaved head, and somewhere he found or stole an old gray fedora that he reconstructed to cover mine. Removing the brim, he serrated the bottom of the crown with scissors and folded it up until it fit my head covering as much as possible of my humiliation.

We wore our caps continuously—even in the house when we could get away with it—but Papa would not allow them at the table. Eating was related in his mind to religion, and the wearing of hats was not respectful in this situation.

Because Papa went off to work early, and Angie and Mike drifted away into the street, I was alone most of the day. It never occurred to me to go back to see the Niccoli boys even though they were just a few blocks away. In those days people often lived their whole lives without venturing more than three or four blocks from their flats. So I was alone, and attempting to entertain myself the day I found the surprise package.

I went down into the dingy basement of our new flat to explore. Moving through the dark unpleasant place, I reached the backyard, where I found a small package wrapped in the jokes (funny papers) and tied with string. Fascinated with comics because we didn't have any in our house, I untied the string very carefully not expecting to find anything inside.

But the impossible materialized: two twenty-dollar bills! I knew because I had learned my numbers at school the previous year. Wealth beyond imagination, and I ran as quickly as possible back to the flat. But, of course, there was no one there to tell, and unable to suppress the news of my good fortune, I went to the kitchen window that opened on to the airshaft and called out.

"I have found money! I have found money! Look here, money wrapped in the jokes."

For a time that seemed like an eternity but was probably only a few seconds, there was no response. Then our neighbor, Maria, appeared at her window above.

"Look," I shouted again this time holding up the money and newspaper. "Look at this money I found."

At first, Maria said nothing, but as the situation began to sink in, she called down to me.

"Wait for me, Johnny. I'll be right down. Wait for me now."

Almost immediately, Maria appeared at our door followed by two other women, all of them anxious to know where I had found the money.

"In the backyard," I said. "right there in the backyard."

"And your Papa," they asked, "where is your Papa?"

"He is selling ice," I informed them wide-eyed at my incredible find. "Papa will not be home until late tonight. What am I gonna do with this money?"

The three young housewives gathered around me inspecting the bills, trying to determine if it was fake money. When they decided it was real, Maria said, "We will help you, little Giovanni. You must give this money to us, and we will go to Macy's and buy something very nice for you."

I was barely six years old and had no one else to advise me, so I gave the three women my treasure.

"Now, you wait right here for us, Giovanni. We will be back soon with your present." they said as they left the flat.

It was two or three hours later before they returned, bearing many boxes. One of the boxes was for me! I danced from foot to foot in anticipation and simultaneously turned my skullcap, scarcely able to contain myself as they opened my package. Maybe it would be a toy or some candy, I thought. When the fact of the package was laid bare before me, my heart sank and my face fell. It was a Little Lord Fauntleroy suit! Black velvet short pants and jacket with a white ruffled shirt. The agony of wildest expectation dashed to bitter disappointment!

But the three housewives were delighted with the suit and insisted upon trying it on me immediately. I could not say no, of course, because adults were not to be refused. The velvet pants went on first, and I knew there was no way that I was going to wear this ridiculous suit. But soon I stood before them in my new outfit. I must have been a sight because it was too small for me: the pants hiked up in the crotch, and the sleeves of the jacket and shirt ended halfway between my wrists and elbows.

After admiring me profusely, Maria and her friends left, taking the rest of the packages with them. For whatever reason, Mike came home before I could get out of the impossible new outfit. I can only surmise his horror on finding me in short pants and ruffles, even though the effect was ameliorated by my beloved skullcap. Mike was a little rough as he helped me off with the new clothes, and did not stop to ask how all of this had come about until I was back to normal in my filthy pants and torn shirt.

"I found two twenty-dollar bills wrapped up in jokes in the backyard, and Maria and her two friends helped me," I explained, daring to cry because I knew Mike would not beat me for bawling.

Mike confronted Maria and her friends, but they insisted that I had found two one-dollar bills and that they had spent all of the money for my perfectly good suit. I never knew what Mike did with it, I only know that I never saw my Little Lord Fauntleroy suit again.

Fox in the Bush and Eggs for Supper

"Johnny," Mike said one day after school, "let's go around the corner and see if we can steal some eggs." Since we had had no breakfast or lunch that day, this sounded like a good idea to me.

"Yeah! If we find some eggs, we can have *fritatta* for supper."

"On the way home from school just now, I saw a truckload of birds pull up in front of the Jewish chicken market," Mike went on. "Maybe they have laid eggs in their cages."

As we rounded the corner of the market, Mike explained how he would climb up the side of the truck and search for eggs while I kept on the lookout.

"If you see anybody coming, holler 'Fox in the bush' and run for home," Mike ordered. I knew how to play Fox in the Bush, because I had been punched in the arm plenty by the first guy to spot a rabbi. As far as we were concerned, any man with a beard was a rabbi, and when the first kid spotted one, he would punch the kid next to him until he, in turn, saw the rabbi and hollered "Fox in the bush!" and punched somebody else in the arm.

"What does 'Fox in the bush' mean?" I asked Mike.

"It means the Jewish rabbis could hide a fox in their long beards."

The rabbi was making the chickens kosher when we arrived. Mike and I were fascinated as he stroked the feathers of the neck against the grain, all the time chanting a prayer, and suddenly slicing the jugular vein and throwing the dying bird into a barrel to flop and bleed to death.

"What's he saying, Mike?" I asked.

"He's making the *bruchas*."

"What's the *bruchas*?"

"The *bruchas* is the Yiddish word for prayer," Mike explained patiently. "It'll be easy for you to remember because you know what *auf dein tuchas* is and *bruchas* rhymes with *tuchas*."

Well, I certainly did know what *auf dein tuchas* meant. In fact, I knew how to say "Up your ass," in three languages: Italian, Yiddish and English.

We watched as the rabbi brought chicken after chicken from the truck and went through his gory ritual. At one point, Mike gave me the eye and wandered around where he could scale up the far side of the truck in search of our supper. I continued to watch the rabbi hoping he wouldn't discover Mike, but when the priest started toward the back of the truck, I hollered, "Fox in the bush!" and ran for home as fast as I could.

The signal worked because Mike got away and caught up with me before I reached the flat. We didn't speak until we were safely inside. Breathless and hungry, I asked,"Did you get some eggs?"

Mike had stuffed them all in his shirt—three small eggs and two large ones.

"What are those big eggs?"

"Those are goose eggs."

"What's a goose?" (I must have been a real trial for my brother at that time, but there was no one else to ask.)

"A big duck. And the Jews eat goose grease on *matzoh*. You know, 'hem-stitched cardboard'."

36

Our feast that night was worth all the trouble we had gone to. Mike and Angie scrambled the stolen eggs with some cheese, Papa put a loaf of Italian bread on the table, and after dinner, we listened to Caruso.

Barbecued Sparrow

Many of my early memories are related to food because we were hungry so much of the time after Mama died, and this memory is no different. I was sitting on the stoop after school watching sparrows in the street as they picked the undigested oats out of horse manure. The late afternoon was pleasantly warm, and I dozed with my skullcapped head in my hands as the birds fluttered and flew.

The idea came out of that place between waking and sleeping where dreams mingle with the everyday world.

"Catch a sparrow and cook it," the dream voice said. By Jesus, it was to be the first time that I would be totally responsible for feeding myself, and my heart raced at the thought. The rest unfolded like a dream, too, because something heretofore unknown inside me knew exactly what to do. I ran around the corner to the chicken market where I found a wooden apple box and a stick. Back on the street in front of our flat, I put the box over an especially large pile of horse droppings and propped one end up with the stick. From our kitchen I brought string which I tied to the stick. Next, I gathered manure in my bare hands and sprinkled it in a line that lead up to my trap.

Now there was nothing to do but wait. The birds continued to chirp and flit in the street but every time a sparrow headed toward my trap it seemed a car would pass. Once the waffle-man went by with his cart and scared a bird nearing the box, and then it was a long time before one began eating oats out of the manure path again. If hunger sharpens the dreams, however, it also sharpens the wits because the moment a bird entered my trap, I had him. Since there was no knife to slit the little creature's throat, and I certainly did not know the *bruchas*, I pulled his head off quite unceremoniously and started plucking the feathers.

By now, a couple of other kids were interested in what I was doing.

"Get matches," I ordered, feeling in command of the situation.

The boys ran off, and when they returned, they not only had matches but two mickies (spuds) as well. We broke up the box for firewood and roasted the sparrow and mickies in the coals and ash.

The spuds were black on the outside and raw on the inside, but we ate them with relish. The boys declined my offer to share the sparrow. The miniscule mouthful of burned flesh and bones did not look very tempting, but my stomach was empty as usual. Also, because I had used my wits to provide it for myself, it tasted especially good to me.

That night, asleep between Angie and Mike, my head at the foot of the bed, I dreamed about birds.

I Find Cheese and Papa is Robbed

The Italian men used to gather across the street at the truck garden on Sunday afternoons to play *bocchia* ball and cards. Here the farmer sold wine for five cents a glass and furnished, free-of-charge, salted *lupino* seeds that increased the men's thirst. I got pretty excited about the *lupino* seeds. of course, because I relished anything in the line of food.

This routine came to an end, however, when a steam shovel was brought to the farm and excavation started for the construction of a large macaroni factory. Each afternoon when I came home from school, I watched them dig the basement. One particular Saturday, I had gotten up early, no breakfast as usual, and taken up my position at the edge of the big hole watching as the steam shovel operators loaded the bottom-dump horse-drawn wagons with dirt.

At noon the shovel crew stopped for lunch, but I stayed on waiting impatiently for them to start work again. About mid-afternoon, the fireman who was also the oiler of the machine came up the bank saying, "Hey kid! Do you want a jelly sandwich?"

Because I had been taught not to take anything from strangers including food or money unless Papa or Mama said it was OK, I refused. The man explained that it was butter and grape jelly, and that it was good for me. Because Mama was no longer there to guide me, I took the sandwich and relished every mouthful of sweetness.

The next Friday afternoon, I went straight from school to the excavation site to see my friends operating the big steam-driven machinery. As soon as I appeared, the fireman led me to a pile of large pear-shaped cheeses that had been unearthed earlier in the day. I recognized them right away as Provolone. Obviously, they were hot cargo that had been stolen from the docks, abandoned in a hurry and buried in the empty field.

"Can I have one?" I asked excitedly.

I Find Cheese and Papa is Robbed

"Kiddo, they're all yours. Take them home."

Wrapped in woven rope carriers, they weighed fifteen or twenty pounds apiece, and I dragged them, two at a time, back to the flat. After telling a neighbor who told other neighbors about my find, I managed to get two more before they all disappeared. Now, we had cheese to eat with our evening loaf of bread which was always served with warm water and olive oil poured over it.

When Papa returned home from work, he told us that the small white maggots we could see in the cheese were good to eat, and I have to admit, they tasted like Provolone. But our good luck that afternoon did not compensate for Papa's bad luck in being held up at gunpoint. It happened just down the street, in front of the cement block plant, that was a cover for a gang of robbers. There were over a dozen or so men in this so-called cement plant. It was known to everyone that when a likely victim came along, they would come out of the office, and rob him at gun point. That day it was Papa's turn, and no one told the police for fear of reprisal.

Mike and I Light a Lamp for a Penny

We were always looking for a way to make money. One Saturday morning Mike said, "Johnny, let's go down to Borough Park and see if we can earn some pennies."

"What do we have to do?"

"Well, the Jews can't light their gas on Saturday, and they'll pay us to do it. All the men down there wear little black skullcaps, have whiskers, and are rabbis. The real young boys are studying to be rabbis, and go to the Jewish school every afternoon to learn Hebrew. Then, when they are thirteen years old, they can be a real rabbi."

I believed every word of my big brother's explanation.

When we got into the Jewish section of town, the appetizing smell of pastrami and corned beef wafted into the street where it mingled with the pungence of pickled cucumbers, tomatoes, and green apples. Here, customers could buy, along with many other mouth-watering treats, a succulent hot meat sandwich spiced with Jewish mustard, and a two-cent sour pickle.

As we walked along New Utrecht Avenue, a rabbi standing in the doorway stopped us and asked, "Will you light the gas for me? I will give you a penny."

Agreeing instantly, we followed the man up a flight of stairs to the flat above his store. In the kitchen we were shown the matches, the gas lamp and the penny which had been placed on the table the day before.

Mike climbed on a chair and lit the lamp, and when he was finished the rabbi said, "Thank you, *kinderla*. There's the penny."

We left happy and rich, but still puzzled why the man could not light his own lamp or touch the penny. On our way home, we stopped at a candy store and bought a cupful of Indian nuts.

Thanksgiving Dinner at Father Appo's

Papa was cleaning the church after mass when he got the word that we were all invited to Father Appo's house for Thanksgiving Dinner. My delight was dampened somewhat, however, when I discovered we would have to go to the new parish house in Williamsburg District by subway. I always got motion sickness on subway trains. And sure enough, I became sick on the train, but it was forgotten the moment we reached our destination. The idea of dinner with Father Appo overshadowed any inconvenience or illness I might have encountered on the way.

Father Locksley Appo opened the door himself and greeted us warmly. After kissing his ring, we three children stood aside to quietly survey the scene. There were nine or ten nuns, the three street kids that Father had taken in to live with him and one other person whom we did not know. She was a tall, beautiful woman who wore lipstick and a wide-brimmed yellow hat. She shone like a bright angel in contrast to the pale nuns in their black habits. Not only did she wear makeup—which was quite unthinkable except for ladies of the night—she was smoking a cigarette in a long gold holder, as well. Papa didn't say anything, of course, but we knew how horrified he must be to see such a woman in Father's house.

When Father introduced the woman as his sister, Papa was even more shocked and could scarcely respond to her pleasant greeting. For even though we had become used to the fact that Father Locksley Appo's lifestyle included expensive chauffeur-driven cars, servants, and lavish dinner parties, we were not prepared for this: a sister dressed in the highest fashion, wearing makeup and smoking! Years later I was to discover that this sister was a fashion writer for a Paris newspaper.

Mike, who was the source of most of my information and misinformation at that time, later explained to me that Father Appo and his sister were Algonquin Indians, and so it was only natural that

40

both of them had dark skin and smoked. Soon our surprise at finding this worldly woman in a parish house gave way to the marvelous smells coming from the kitchen. We did not speak to the other boys until we sat down to dinner because we were on our very best behavior and knew we should be quiet.

There were two tables set in the large dining room, one for grown-ups and one for us kids. The roast suckling pig that was brought to our table was so far beyond my wildest imagination that I recall nothing else about that Thanksgiving dinner. It had an apple in its open mouth and glistened golden with grease.

"The insides are still in it," Mike gasped in wide-eyed disbelief. "It's a whole pig."

Beyond that there was little conversation at the children's table. We ate what we were served, and I felt a little sick because I was not used to so much or such rich food. And maybe Papa's stomach suffered from the generous feast, too, because that evening on the subway, he let a great fart that was heard all through our half of the car. Breaking wind was quite acceptable in Italy, and Papa smiled broadly as though he had just announced his contentment to the people around us. But Angie and Mike knew farting was not socially acceptable in America and were humiliated.

"Shame on you, Papa," Angie scolded. "You mustn't do that. People don't like it."

The more Angie said, the more delighted Papa became, and the more everyone around us laughed, cheered-up by Papa's overt flatulence. I had been told not to break wind in school, but like Papa, I felt it was OK to fart anyplace else and joined him in announcing our full stomachs to the occupants of our subway car. That evening as we left the train, Papa led me by the hand, but Mike and Angie, embarrassed, walked about fifty feet ahead.

A Night to Remember: A Hunchbacked Lamplighter;
Another Stabbing; A Crystal Set; And Margarita

Winter was coming on and it was cold the evening Mike and I set out to visit one of his friends back on 65th Street who had a crystal-set radio. Since this would be my first experience of hearing one, I was very excited. We wore long red sweaters that hung halfway to our knees, drew our necks down into the wool of the collars and walked along briskly until we came upon a hunchbacked lamplighter at work. Watching as the crippled man propped the small ladder

41

against the lamppost, I remembered Mama telling us to always be respectful of ill-formed people and never ridicule them. Maybe Mike was remembering, too, because we both stood there quietly and thoughtfully as the old man struck a match and lighted the gas lamp.

Around us, people hurried home with their evening groceries. We followed the lamplighter as he carried the ladder on his shoulder to the next post, watching as he went through his ritual again, fascinated by his work and his misshapen body, feeling sympathy. It was as though we formed a trio, the hunchback, Mike and I, a small island of caring in the evening rush. Perhaps the lamplighter felt it, too, because he paused to show us how his ladder narrowed at the top to be just the right size to rest against the post horns.

"And when I get to the top, I hang onto the horns, so I don't fall while I strike the match," he explained, pointing upward without looking because it was difficult for him to lift his head out of the hump. "I have to start while it is still daytime if I am to get all of the lamps lighted by dark."

Before either of us had time to respond, an open touring car with two men in the back seat pulled up to the curb. They were swearing at each other in Italian. The driver paid no attention, looking straight ahead as though totally unaware of what was going on. As the argument escalated, one man called the other a "son of a bitch." At that, the men rather matter-of-factly got out of the car and began swinging at each other. The lamplighter moved on, and so did the people around us, but before we got away, one man reached for his back pocket. He pulled out a switchblade, started cutting up the other man, and when the wounded man slumped to the pavement, the attacker got back into the car and commanded, *"Presto!"*

As we looked back, people coming upon the scene seemed to flow around the dead man on the street like water flows around a log in the river. And by the time we reached Mike's friend, we had all but forgotten the incident ourselves.

Carlucci had a room of his own where the small magic crystal set loomed large under the only light. Because he was very selective about who he invited to come and listen to the dry-cell operated instrument, Mike and I sat quietly and reverently while he tuned it.

"There's a man talking," he said at last, passing the earphones to Mike who listened for a moment before handing them to me.

At first all I heard was static, but then, slowly, I could make out a voice. Because I could not understand how those words came through the air, I felt certain the boys were playing a trick on me and had a phonograph connected to this device. Nevertheless, I was awestruck at having heard my first radio.

The excitement of this evening was not to end there. When we got back home, Papa and Angie were in the kitchen washing up. This was surprising in itself, but we were further surprised when we, too, were instructed to wash our hands and faces, and comb our hair.

"Why are we cleaning up, Papa?" I asked, confused at this turn of events. After all, I had washed my face that morning, and I did not want to burn my eyes with strong soap twice in one day.

"Your new mama is coming tonight," he explained, and that news further stunned us three kids. We objected, but were overruled as Papa went on, "It's the only chance I have to keep us all together. Signora Yolanda, the go-between, has already met with me, and tonight she brings a woman just off the boat from Italy to marry me."

Immediately, Angie and I started crying, "We don't want a new Mama," as the tears ran down our clean faces.

"*Silenzio!*" Papa commanded, "The two ladies will be here any minute now." And true to his prediction, the women arrived almost immediately.

As Papa opened the door, Signora Yolanda, a large imposing woman, pushed the intended bride into the kitchen ahead of her. I could see nothing but a dark pinched face peering out from beneath a black shawl draped over a black dress. The whole dimly-lit scene was very dismal, and we three kids stood silently in a row as Papa introduced us to the ladies as "my children." Bypassing further niceties, Yolanda, who was experienced and all business, immediately began selling the virtues of this stranger to Papa.

"Margarita will make a wonderful wife. As you can see, she is very little and doesn't eat much, so she will not be expensive to support. Also, she worked hard on the farm in Italy and is very strong."

Margarita hung her head and said nothing.

Papa did not seem to be any more impressed than we kids with the sad-looking woman who must have felt like a chattel as she stood in front of us, waiting. Possibly, he was considering her as a new mama for our sakes more than as a wife for himself, and that was why he turned to the three of us little ones asking, "Would you like this woman to be your mama?"

In spite of the fact that we knew our rejection of her might mean the family would have to split up, we answered in unison with a loud, "No!" We could detect the relief on Papa's face because our feelings gave him the out he wanted. Turning to Margarita, he

43

gestured sadness with open hands and announced that there would be no wedding.

"I am sorry, but my children still miss their mama too much. I cannot marry you," Papa said sadly.

His decision meant no money for Yolanda and no husband for Margarita. Even so, the women did not argue.

When they left, we were all relieved in spite of the fact that a family split was again looming. We knew for sure that we wouldn't have been happy with the miserable woman who was willing to sell herself as a family caretaker in exchange for food and lodging. What we didn't know for certain was what adventures or misadventures lay ahead if we had to break up.

We Go Our Separate Ways

Within a week, Father Appo made arrangements for Angie to be placed in a Catholic girls' home. She was crying as she packed her few belongings and kissed us goodbye, not knowing whether she would ever see us again. Waving out the back window of Father Appo's Dodge sedan, she watched us standing on the sidewalk, waving back, until the car disappeared around the corner.

The plan for Mike was that he would go live with Father McCarthy and study to become a priest. Mike was actually looking forward to going because he still remembered the Thanksgiving dinner with all the food and the other boys that Father Appo was raising. But this was not to be because, within a week of Mike's scheduled move, Father McCarthy died. There was nothing, at the moment, for Mike but to stay with Papa.

And then it was my turn. Papa didn't say anything until the next Sunday morning when he announced, "Come on, Johnny. We're gonna visit Pat in Suffern." Pat had recovered from his bout with tuberculosis. Released from the sanatorium, he had remained in Suffern and married a local woman.

I had mixed emotions about going. I wanted to see my brother—but I also knew I would be sick on the train. Papa saw to it that I sat next to the window facing the direction we were going, so that helped. The forty-mile journey north was a new experience for me because I had never been so far from home. Since we were traveling through heavily industrialized areas, however, about all I saw on either side was the flash of dirty windows in dingy brownstone factories. But what I heard—oh, that was exciting. The eerie sound of the whistle, the rapid clang of the crossing bell, and the synco-pated "click-click, click-click" of the wheels on the track.

When we arrived in Suffern, we found it was a short walk to the flat where Pat lived with his new wife and baby. They were surprised to see us because Papa had no way of letting them know we were coming. Nevertheless, they seemed mildly pleased and Louisa started to prepare dinner.

I didn't pay much attention to the conversation, because I was too busy looking out the window at the tree-covered hills that were strange to me. But suddenly, something Papa said caught my attention.

"Giovanni is a good boy, and I will pay you, of course."

It began to dawn on me! Papa intended to leave me here with Pat and Louisa in these strange surroundings.

"There is a woman in this house, and Giovanni needs a mama," Papa went on.

At first Pat and his wife said nothing. They were obviously not thrilled at the thought of taking me in.

"Are you going to leave me here, Papa?" I got up from the table and went to stand by him.

"Yes, Giovanni, but just for a short while. I will come and get you as soon as I can."

"He will have to mind and do everything just as we tell him," Pat said. "Louisa is busy caring for me and the baby."

No one asked me if I wanted to stay or go, and when it was agreed how much and when Papa would pay, he kissed me goodbye and left. I felt numb inside like an empty package that had been dropped off on the doorstep of people who did not want it. Soon, Louisa brought me a blanket and showed me where I could sleep on the davenport.

Alone at the window that night long after the others had gone to bed, I thought of Papa and wondered when he would return for me. Lying down at last, I drew the blanket under my chin and shuddered in terror as the screaming trains came and went on the main Chicago-New York line. Beginning as far-off wails, the locomotives approached full-throttle and seemed to enter our very flat, brutal, belching, bell-ringing monsters that obliterated me completely on their way through. They destroyed me, wiped me out for the time it took them to pass and fade down the tracks. In the short lull between engines, I drifted off but could not really sleep for another whistle would soon begin to mourn in the distance.

3

From the City to the Country

Many Changes—Even My Name

In Brooklyn the only dangerous animals we encountered were human animals, and I had managed, somehow, to avoid harm from them. Here in rural Suffern, however, I had to be on the look-out for other kinds of dangerous animals: rattlesnakes, copperheads, and water moccasins. And there were many other differences as well. The "mountains," as we called the gentle Ramapo Hills, were in considerable contrast to the flat slender sandbar of Long Island, where we could look directly from Brighton Beach to the skyscrapers of midtown Manhattan about ten miles away. Here, our view was confined by the hills enclosing the Ramapo Valley, through which ran the Ramapo River and the Erie Railroad lines connecting New York to Chicago.

There were many trees in Brooklyn in those days, including the big poplar split by lightning outside the flat where Mama died, but all of those trees had been planted for shade and pleasure. In Suffern, the trees were native and included the pines that covered the hills and many varieties of nut trees, such as butternut, black walnut, hickory and pig nut, scattered across the hills and throughout the valley. And though it may seem surprising, there were more cars in Suffern than there had been in Brooklyn because the distances people had to travel were greater. In Brooklyn a horse and wagon still served to get pedlars and business men where they needed to go, and only the gangsters and wealthy had automobiles. In Suffern, however, automobiles and trucks were required by almost everyone to go to work or to drive to adjoining towns, so the streets were busy with the traffic of Marmons, Fords, Stars, Moons, Durants, Whippets, and many other early models. Even my brother Pat had a Chevy panel truck that he used in his laundry business.

Perhaps the greatest changes I encountered were within the

family. Suddenly, there were three meals a day, and though not bountiful, they were regular. Always, a piece of buttered toast and coffee for breakfast; boiled beans for lunch; and different pasta dishes for supper. And though this was a great improvement for me once my stomach became adjusted to receiving so much more food, there were drawbacks as well. For instance, while Papa had paid little attention to our table manners, Louisa and Pat took it upon themselves to teach me a certain amount of finesse. Their methods were direct and employed surprise attack. The first slap for slurping my spaghetti took me completely unawares and nearly knocked me off my chair. But I must admit the approach worked to improve my manners rather quickly—although it did not do much to endear me to the two of them, who were not crazy about having me around anyway. It seemed to me that even little Victor did not like me very much; because though he was only two, he took great pleasure in kicking me from his high chair during meals. I complained about the bruises, but Pat and Louisa refused to move him to the other end of the table where he would be unable to reach me. Probably, they took a covert delight in Victor's kicks because he was doing what they wished they could do.

And so, I learned not to ask for anything in this period. I believed I was not supposed to have things. If I was cold, I did not ask for clothes. If I was hungry, I did not ask for food. Once I saw an erector set that I wanted very badly in a store window, but a deep sense of resignation to my lot in life kept me from thinking further about it.

Even my name changed when I went to live in Suffern. At the time I did not understand why Pat enrolled me as Tursi (as he spelled his name) rather than Torccio, as I had been known in Brooklyn. Of course, I did not question Pat at the time because I had learned my lesson well and did as I was told without questioning. It was not until many years later that I learned from Tony why each of us kids had a different family name.

When a child was born, the midwife filling out the birth certificate would ask Papa what the child's name was. With great gusto Papa then held up the new baby and declared its name. The midwife would ask how to spell it, but, of course, Papa could neither read nor write, so he would just pronounce the name proudly and loudly once again, and the poor midwife spelled it the best she could. She would then show the paper to Papa and ask him if that was right. He would agree, though he didn't know one letter from the other, and a baby could have been named "hot dog" for all he realized.

Small wonder that all six of us had different family names on our birth certificates: Torccio, Torrcio, Tursy, Torcci, Turci, and Tursi.

And so I started school with a new name in a new town. I was now John Tursi, who lived with his brother in Suffern and attended a big two-story building under the principalship of grouchy Beatrice Patchin, who did not allow us to talk during recess (which mainly consisted of lining up in the hall to use the lavatory). My only other memory of Miss Patchin is of the day her slip straps broke, and that undergarment ended up draped over her shoes as she monitored us in line. After her initial shock, she hurriedly stepped out of it, swooped it up, and headed like a ship under full sail for the teachers' room.

All Work and Little Play

After school and all day Saturday I worked behind the counter in my brother's laundry receiving dirty clothes and dispensing clean ones. Up front where I was, there were shelves and a couple of ironing boards. In the back there was a small dark room with clotheslines and portable kerosene heaters where items to be ironed—mostly men's shirts—were dried.

Pat picked up laundry in his truck all around Suffern, in the nearby towns of Tuxedo Park, Arden and Slotesberg. These clothes were taken to Ramsey where they were tumbled in large perforated wooden cylinders that rotated slowly in troughs of hot soapy water and spun dry. These "rough dried" clothes were then delivered back to customers or brought to the store to be completely dried in the drying room and ironed.

On Sundays my job was to cut and split kindling so the coal fire in the cookstove could be started easily. I worked in the basement dungeon by candlelight on logs of hardwood—usually oak—sawing away with a handsaw from which many teeth were missing and then splitting them with a dull hatchet.

Not long after arriving, however, I got a paying job—two dollars a week for washing dishes six days at Cerveri's Ice Cream parlor. They always saved the lunch dishes for me, so I arrived as soon as possible after school and worked until seven in the evening, tempted and tantalized by even the second-hand smell of chocolate from the used cups. For all of the time I worked there, I was never offered any ice cream or candy, and felt I could not spend any of my earnings on such luxury. Instead, I bought clothes and a two-dollar piccolo with

48

my money. I became so proficient on my new instrument that I was soon asked to play "Barcarole" at the Friday assembly at school. Soon after that, the piccolo turned up missing, and to this day I do not know if it was stolen or used for kindling. Whatever happened, I always blamed it on a poor performance.

Usually, I had a few hours free on Sunday afternoon, and early in November about seven or eight of us gathered at Lake Antrim to test the ice. We confiscated a long plank from the Ward Company Rock Quarry and slid it out onto the frozen lake. I picked up a large rock and walked to the outer end of the plank with the rest of the boys following. Dropping the rock on the rubbery ice, I was shocked to see water boiling up through the test hole that opened at my feet. I yelled for the others to go back, but before I could turn around, we were all submerged and scrambling over one another to reach the safety of the lakeshore.

We were all safe but terrified and shivering in the sub-zero cold. "Let's go to the asphalt plant and ask the man if we can come in and warm up," someone suggested through blue lips. When we appeared at the door, the man was so shocked to see the bedraggled, frozen lot of us that he invited us in immediately. We scrambled atop the steam boiler and stayed there until we were warm and dry. I went home that evening, little the worse for wear, happy to be alive even if I would have to explain the soiled clothes.

Later during the winter when the ice reached a safe thickness, I went ice skating on Lake Antrim using a pair of old clamp-ons that had been given to me. It was like nothing I had ever experienced, and at first when I heard the ice crack on expanding, I was afraid it would open, and I would be swallowed up again. As I came to trust the frozen waters, however, I always struggled against the prevailing wind to the head of the lake where I opened my coat and spread out my arms. I became a winged boy and swept downwind through the bitter cold to the other end, swooping and flapping like a large clumsy bird.

On other occasions all of us kids would form a whip, skate in a circle, and the last person would cut loose and be propelled half-way across the lake. And though I usually went on my back and not the skates, the minor pain that might accrue was well worth the fun.

Some Sunday afternoons I would fish through a hole in the ice, but I never caught anything. Other times I would watch as workers sawed great blocks of ice and poled them to the conveyor that moved them into a huge ice house to be stored for summer.

It was in Suffern that I became a practicing Catholic. Back in Brooklyn the main connection to the church had been Father Appo's kindly hand on my uncombed hair as he asked, "And how are you, Giovanni my boy?" I never attended mass or Sunday school.

Now, I was glad to follow Pat and Louisa's dictum that I had to attend church and Sunday school every week, Attending to religion gave me a feeling of belonging—something I badly needed. Suffern had a population of about three thousand at that time, and the good-sized Catholic church was so full during the two regular masses that kids had to sit in the balcony and sing in the choir. Maybe I had a good voice, because sometimes the rest of the kids were silent as I sang under the leader's direction. I didn't notice I was singing solos at first, because I was so eager to please that all my attention was focused on the director.

After mass I went with the other kids to Sunday school in the parochial building. Here, too, I paid attention and was anxious to participate. One morning the teacher asked what we knew about Adam's apple—at least that's what I thought she said.

My hand flew up and when I was recognized I rose to recite. "Adam took a bite of the apple, and it got stuck in his throat and that's why men have Adam's apples," I explained proudly. Perhaps this was information I had received from brother Mike.

The kids laughed, the nuns frowned and I was embarrassed because I thought the answer had been perfectly acceptable. Sitting down puzzled and hurt, I hung my head as the jollity continued around me. It was then that my favorite nun, Sister Karen, a young bright-eyed woman full of laughter and enthusiasm, came to my rescue.

"All right, now children, that's enough. John gave the answer that he thought was right. You must not laugh at him," she said walking over and putting her hand on my shoulder.

In spite of the ridicule by others, her kindness made me even more eager to study and learn and belong to the church. I memorized the first catechism quickly, keeping it with me and studying every spare moment, greatly anticipating my first communion. The night before this solemn occasion, I went to confession. I was a little scared in the dark cubicle, the priest's voice floating out through the wicket quizzing me about my sins, and the questions took me by surprise:

"How many times have you taken the name of the Lord in vain?"

"How many times have you lied?"

"How many times have you stolen?"

I was crestfallen; I had no sins to confess, or so it seemed. I would never have taken the name of the Lord in vain. The very worst epithet we could fling was "Madonna," and not even a street kid like me would do that except under the direst of conditions. I knew I had lied and stolen, but those things occurred distantly in Brooklyn and did not seem to apply to this situation, so I left my first confession with a feeling of complete failure, determined to do better next time.

I carried my sorrow with me the next day as I marched down the aisle to receive first communion. But it was more than what I perceived as failure at confession that saddened me; there was no one in the church who was there just for me. I wore a tie given me by one of the nuns, and I thought it might choke me; I was that lonely for Mama and Papa.

The KKK—Koons, Kikes, and Katholics

Tony Cataneesi (Cat Knees) was my best friend, and though I worked so much that we couldn't spend a lot of time together, we met one Sunday after dinner to take a hike.

"Let's go up the mountain to see King Tut's head," he suggested.

"Who's King Tut?"

"You'll see," he said with an air of mystery that piqued my curiosity.

"OK, let's go!" My heart raced at the thought of adventure.

The afternoon was warm with sun and bright with fall leaves that rustled and crunched as we climbed.

"Watch out for copperheads, " Tony warned as we climbed. "They are the same color as these leaves, and copperheads can rear right up and bite through your pants."

For a while, I wished I was back in Brooklyn, but my fears subsided when we reached King Tut's head. It was a disappointment: nothing but a great granite boulder with a head chiseled into it—a round circle with eyes and nose like kids make when they first begin drawing.

"What's so great about this?" I wanted to know.

"Well, nobody knows how he got here. He's a king from Egypt or someplace," Tony explained, attempting to perk up our adventure. "Come on, let's go to the top. Papa said the Ku Kluckers are up to something for election day."

I vaguely knew about the Ku Kluckers. Mr. Johnson in the flat below ours was one. I had seen him leave for KKK meetings wearing his white hood and robes. When I asked Pat about it, he said KKK stood for Koons, Kikes, and Katholics—and that Ku Kluckers hated them. Now, the afternoon was moving in the direction of excitement again as we scrambled upward once more.

It wasn't long before we found the stimulation we were looking for. Coming suddenly upon a large flat outcropping of rock, we stood wide-eyed for a few seconds trying to comprehend what we saw. Quickly we realized that we had stumbled upon what was to become a KKK burning rite. There on the rock before us lay a big Christian cross and three large Ks made of wood wrapped in burlap sacks, and several five-gallon cans of kerosene. We knew that one of those Ks stood for Katholic, and that meant us.

"We've gotta get out of here quick. If the Ku Kluckers find us, they'll kill us," Tony gasped.

And we were off in a flurry of fright and leaves, pell-mell down the trail, helter-skelter over fallen trees and rocks, when suddenly Tony stopped and grabbed my arm as I stumbled past.

"Hold it!" he cried. "There's a copperhead!" And sure enough, a camouflaged snake slithered through the colored leaves at our feet. Tumbling on in increasing terror, we flew by King Tut without so much as doffing our caps.

At the bottom of the hill, walking toward main street, we tried to appear casual, a little embarrassed at being so scared, feeling safer, now, among the houses and people. Before separating that afternoon, we agreed to meet downtown on Tuesday evening for the election celebration.

The year was 1926, and Roman Catholic Al Smith was making his fourth bid for governor against Ogden Mills. I had heard talk about the Ku Kluckers hating Smith but was not prepared for what happened that election evening. Cat Knees and I were enjoying the spectacle of cars driving slowly up and down the streets, horns honking and people waving. The next best thing to a parade! The atmosphere was friendly and festive, especially down toward the polling booth, where we were headed when the mysterious blast occurred.

Cat Knees and I were among the first to locate the source. Perhaps our Sunday encounter caused us to look up at the mountains. There on the hillside were the three "Ks" and the cross we had seen earlier, raging in hate and fire. Apparently the Ku Kluckers had set off dynamite to draw the attention of the crowd to their noxious statement, but before people could completely grasp what was going on, pandemonium broke out elsewhere in Suffern.

"The Catholic church is on fire," came the shouts echoing along the street, as the crowd began running in that direction. Tony and I also ran toward the church, which was directly across the street from the monument in honor of all those who served in World War I. We could see a yellowish-glow reflected in the stained glass windows, and soon realized the church itself was not on fire. Instead, just ahead on the church lawn, a flaming cross burned its threatening message into the night sky.

As we stood there, terrified about what the Klansmen were going to do next, Police Chief Lenny roared up on his motorcycle. Racing across the grass, he knocked over the burning cross with his puttee-covered shoes and kicked it onto the sidewalk where it was left to burn out harmlessly.

"Let's get away from here," I whispered to Tony. For though the incident had not turned out to be all that dangerous, we were two scared kids. We feared that the Klansmen knew we had discovered their paraphernalia in preparation of this harassment, and if we were found here, they might kidnap us and tie us to a burning cross.

Before Tony could answer, the curfew warning sounded, and we knew it was fifteen minutes before nine o'clock. We separated, and I worried all the way home for fear a passing car would stop, a white-hooded man would grab me, and I would be spirited away. After all, I was a Katholic.

The Jackson Whites

"Hee loo, kid," the two long-haired men said.

"Hello." I tried not to look too surprised by their unusual appearance. Both of them wore filthy tweed caps stretched down over their ears and dirty brown pullovers that appeared to have never been washed; each carried a bundle of beaver and muskrat pelts. They were on their way to Suffern, where they would sell the furs to buy staples and get their annual haircuts.

This father and son were Jackson Whites, members of a minor group that developed in the Ramapo Hills from an intermixture of British, blacks and Native Americans. For the most part, they kept to themselves except for annual trips out with their furs. The most widely accepted idea concerning their origin is that, during Colonial times, one Captain Jackson provided women for the British forces in

New York. Some of these women were white and some were black, so in the beginning they were known as Jackson Blacks as well as Jackson Whites. When the British left New York, both the black and white women found their way north and intermarried with whites and Indians, finally coming to be known as Jackson Whites.

As a youngster, I knew none of this history and still remember my wonder and awe whenever I saw these interesting-looking people. They were of high yellow complexion and often had coarse features with prominent cheekbones and wide-spaced teeth. They lived scattered throughout the Eagle and Ramapo valleys and were generally shunned as outcasts because they were of mixed blood.

On this particular day, my fascination with them faded quickly because as we walked along the sidewalk near the railroad spur, a locomotive pulled up, and Mr. Kelly, the engineer who lived in our building, offered me a ride into town in the cab. Of course, the Jackson Whites were not invited because they were different from the rest of us.

I was ecstatic when the fireman reached down and pulled me up into the great machine that hissed and puffed as it paused for me. It seemed unreal that I should be able to ride into Suffern, or anywhere for that matter, on this monstrous locomotive with its huge black wheels and tremendous power. The Jackson Whites were impressed, too, I supposed. They stood wide-eyed watching me steam into the distance as I waved to them from the cab of what all of us kids called the "choo-choo."

Since none of my friends saw me on the locomotive, and because it was such an improbability that little Johnny Tursi would ever have ridden on one, nobody believed me when I told them. In my heart, however, there was a secret bond between me and the two Jackson White men. They *knew* I had had a ride on a "choo choo."

Oxheart Cherries and a Film of the Arctic

In those days the Boy Scouts of America was not for kids like me: boys who did not have money or position. And although Dan Beard, National Scout Commissioner from 1910 to his death in 1941, lived on an estate outside of Suffern, I never even dreamed of becoming a Boy Scout. I did visit his orchard, however, one summer when the Oxheart cherries were ripe.

Cat Knees and I went over the fence and up one of the big trees and sat enjoying the luscious fruit when Uncle Dan spotted us. He came running across the orchard, shotgun in hand, hollering at us to get out of his tree. We lost no time getting out of there. I could never be sure that this fine old humanitarian would have actually shot at us, but, even so, I never forgot that the cherries probably went to waste and could have just as well been shared with us.

Later, the word was around that the Arctic explorer Captain Robert Bartlett would show motion pictures of his recent expedition to the Boy Scouts of Suffern. Several of us got together and decided to try to look in through the window of the community hall across the street from the church.

We took up our positions and tried to be very quiet so we would not be sent away. One of the Boy Scouts saw our faces at the window, however, and told good old Uncle Dan who immediately wanted to shoo us away. Captain Bartlett had another idea: he discussed the matter with the group and they responded by inviting us in for the program. The only stipulation was that we keep quiet and act like gentlemen, and we were happy to do that because the pictures were rare and a great treat for us.

My Indiscreet Nun and More About Confession

I was beginning the advanced catechism class when I saw a most puzzling thing. I had been given permission to go to the bathroom, and left the room quietly and slowly because, like many kids, I was in no great hurry to get back to the lesson. Dreamily walking along on rubber-soled sneakers, I paused briefly at the pipe-railed stairwell that led to the basement and looked down. There she was, my favorite nun, Sister Karnelina, in a most un-nun-like situation.

She stood with eyes closed embracing and kissing the church usher. I was astounded, as I knew that nuns did not kiss men or marry. But there she was, her habit partially raised exposing white legs that probably seldom, if ever, saw the light of day. The dark, curly-haired usher held her buttocks in his large, powerful hands as they swayed rhythmically, unaware that anyone was watching.

I didn't comprehend exactly what was going on, but I somehow knew it was a forbidden situation, so I slipped away without being heard or seen. When I returned from the bathroom, I gave the stairwell a wide berth, but I could see they were still kissing. Now, I was more confused about religion than ever before, and it took many years for me to realize that the religious community was as human as any other.

And, of course, I continued to go to confession myself, and because I wanted so much to be a good Catholic, I looked forward to this Saturday night ritual. After my first disappointing experience when I felt I had no sins to confess, I soon learned to lie to please the priest.

"Have you used the Lord's name in vain?" he asked.

" Yes. Ten or fifteen times," I lied.

"Have you stolen?"

"No, Father," I lied again, not wanting to admit even to myself that I had stolen cherries.

"Have you masturbated?"

"What's 'masturbate'?"

There was a deep silence and Father moved on to the next question without explaining.

"How many times have you lied?"

"I lied ten times, Father," I said, continuing to lie.

All of this sinning required me to do fifteen "Our Fathers" and twenty-five "Hail Marys." I felt that lying during confession was making me a very good Catholic.

I Won't Eat Beans and Get a Beating

Beatings were not unusual for me at this age of seven, and for that matter, neither were other types of punishment. One of the more unusual disciplinings that I received at the hands of my sister-in-law came when I was jerked out of bed on a bitterly cold morning and made to stand outside in my long johns because I had forgotten to bring kindling up from the basement. I huddled on the outside landing, barefoot and numb with cold, peered in the window as she built the fire and hoped I would soon be allowed back inside. The punishment worked because I never forgot to bring up the kindling again.

But the most memorable beating that I received came about because I refused to eat a plate of tasteless beans. It was Wednesday noon and every Wednesday lunch was the same, beans. Louisa was not the cook that my mother had been, and somewhere I must have remembered Mama's *pasta fazoola* spicy with garlic, parsley, oregano, rosemary and olive oil. And every Wednesday, when I sat down to Louisa's plain boiled beans awash in the juice of plum tomatoes, my taste buds rebelled.

On this particular day the food just would not go down. I moved

56

the hated beans one by one around my plate, stalling in the hope that I would not have to eat them.

"Why aren't you eating?" Louisa asked.

"I don't like the beans," I said, hanging my head.

"Why don't you find another place to eat?"

The courage for my answer came from somewhere deep inside.

"OK! I will!" I got up from the table and left for school.

The next day I had forgotten the incident when I sat down with the others for lunch.

"I thought you were going to find another place to eat," Louisa said angrily.

I didn't know what to feel. I was embarrassed and at the same time angry at myself. I had not followed through with my threat to eat elsewhere and I had been called on it. My pride was bent as I walked hungry and dejected back to school, where I watched the kids kicking a soccer ball around the playground until it was time for afternoon classes to begin. As I entered the school, I saw my teacher standing there with a look of horror and helplessness on her face. My brother was waiting for me behind the door, and grabbed me by the back of the neck.

"What's the matter?" I cried.

"Never mind 'what's the matter'," he said as he pushed me toward the truck and shoved me inside.

I knew, as my teacher had known, that a beating was coming, and nothing I could say or do would change that fact. Neither of us said a word as he drove to the laundry, dragged me past a horrified employee, and hurried me into the drying room.

"You don't like beans, huh?" he snarled with a half-grin on his face, as he began beating and kicking me. Each time I fell to the floor, he pulled me up and stood me against the wall, so he could beat me some more.

"I won't say anything about the food anymore. Please stop beating me," I cried.

"You stop crying now, and I will decide when you've had enough." he continued, punching and slapping me around. I covered my head with my arms and hands as best I could, being particularly concerned for my teeth and ears as the blows continued. When he knocked me down, I pulled myself toward the protection of a corner of the room but soon realized the brutal kicks were more painful than the hand beating.

I finally knew that I had to stop crying no matter how much it hurt, and when, at last, I managed to quench the tears and swallow my sobs, he stopped and walked out, but not until he delivered one final blow to my head that nearly knocked me unconscious. I fell into a heap on the floor, emotionally and physically bruised, hurting all over. The only light that came into the room was from the transom above the door and I lay for a long time in the half-dark remembering there was something called The American Society for Prevention of Cruelty to Animals and wondering if there wasn't anybody who cared about the prevention of cruelty to boys.

Several days later, Pat told me coldly that he had made arrangements for me to ride with a truck driver to Manhattan. He was sending me back to Papa. There was no time to say goodbye to my friends or to check out of school. As I climbed into the cab of the dark-green Reo truck, relieved to be leaving my brother and anticipating seeing Papa, Pat handed me a slip of paper with an address in Brooklyn. Otherwise, I was empty-handed. I didn't own so much as a toothbrush and had no spare clothes to worry about.

I was happy to be riding in a truck, fascinated with the small towns we passed through on our way. Dingy, soot-blackened towns on the Jersey side of the Hudson: Hohokus, Ridgewood, Paterson, Passaic, Rutherford and Jersey City. When we reached the Holland Tunnel, the driver told me to get into the back because he could not pay the toll for me. I huddled in a corner where I hoped the police would not see me in case they decided to look.

Once safely through the tunnel, the driver stopped and let me out.

"This is the end of the line, kiddo," he said as I stood alone on the street wondering which direction to go. There I was, nine years old, hungry, not a nickel to my name, alone in Manhattan with only an address on a small slip of paper.

4

Back to Brooklyn and No Papa

A Walk to Brighton Beach

I was hesitant to ask a cop how to get to Papa's since I was out of school on a school day, but there was nothing else to be done. He directed me to the Brooklyn Bridge through Chinatown. The smells that rose from the sand on the cobblestone streets were different from the smells of Suffern and pleasantly familiar to me. The large handcut cobbles, slightly rounded on top and a menace to horses, were deeply set in beds of sand that trapped horse urine and manure, fish juice, and all manner of rotten and decaying fruits and vegetables from the street's commerce. This mixture blended to create a sweet-sour odor that pervaded the area and reminded me of Brooklyn. Although it was late morning, I imagined danger behind every door, trouble lurking around each corner.

Since Papa and I had visited his sister in Chinatown once, I vaguely knew about Tong wars and the dreaded Tombs prison. Preoccupied by the potential danger, I inadvertently passed the bridge approach and found myself on the waterfront. There I became fascinated by art students, who sat beneath the high arches of the bridge painting the red brick tenements that stretched along the streets in front of them. Admiring their talent, I lingered awhile, watching a woman with a large bandana tied around her head as she transferred the street scene to her canvas. When I finally realized I had better continue my journey before the warring Chinese Tongs kidnapped me, I asked her how to get on the bridge and learned I would have to retrack several blocks.

Finding the approach at last, I stopped in disbelief at the great bridge that swung from cables across the East River. The footwalk on which I was to cross was high and precarious, and there was no other person on it. I wondered if this was the right way to cross, and if, indeed, the cables would hold me. The deck that lay at my feet was constructed of widely-spaced 2 by 6's set so far apart that I felt I might slip through them to the water below. To make matters worse, vibrations created by the train cars and trucks roaring beneath constantly shook the catwalk beneath my feet. At nine years old what lay before me was a test of my ability to survive because I could not turn back. Scared as I was, I knew I had to cross that bridge by myself if I was ever to reach the safety of Papa. Even my stomach told me I had to go; the sun overhead said it was nearly noon, now, and I was getting hungrier and hungrier. The delicious fragrance of freshly roasting coffee from the A & P plant on the Brooklyn side of the Hudson drifted across the river, adding to my hunger pangs.

For the first time in my life I was so high in the air that I could look down on the tenement rooftops with all of their pigeon coops. Pigeon flying was the means of entertainment for many of the men in this stone jungle, and far below me I watched as a man with a long bamboo pole chased his flock into the air, hoping to attract a stray bird.

Continuing on in near-blind terror, I somehow managed to move one foot ahead of the other until I reached the high center. Now I was relieved to realize the supports were strong enough to hold me and to see firm ground at the other end of the span. Safely across at last, I knew I had faced danger and overcome it.

By early evening I reached the Banner Avenue address on my paper. I was excited, expecting to see Papa. But brother Tony answered the door, and he was as surprised to see me as I was to see him and a new wife.

"What are you doing here, Johnny?"

"Pat told me that Papa lived here."

"Papa doesn't live here. I'm not sure where he is." My heart sank.

It was decided that I should spend the night before going on to find Papa, so a bed was made for me on the davenport, and again I found myself at a brother's house where I had not been expected. But unlike the first night at Pat's, there were no trains wailing outside. Instead, the sirens of emergency vehicles filled my head with their urgent comings and goings. However, exhaustion prevailed, and I fell asleep dreaming of dangerous Chinese in high places.

In the morning Tony told me that I could stay for a while and enroll in the new yellow-brick school at Brighton Beach until Papa was located. This was the first of many times to come that I enrolled myself. The principal accepted my word as to what grade I should be in and assigned me to a class. I was scarcely settled in at school when Tony heard that Papa was working for Cousin LaPoppola who lived at the old Sheepshead Bay racetrack just a couple of miles away.

The Happiest Time of My Childhood

But Papa was not at LaPoppola's either, and again I found myself on a doorstep where I was not expected. This time seemed different, however, because they were glad to see me and wanted me to stay.

"Little Giovanni!" Cousin LaPoppola exclaimed when he realized who I was. "I have not seen your Papa for months. He was here in the winter, but now he is gone. But you must stay with us. We have a lot of room in this big house."

Their "big house" was actually the former hospital facility for the now defunct Sheepshead Bay racetrack. The wooden multi-gabled building was home for not only Cousin LaPoppola's family but for his brother's family and the matriarch, Serafina, as well. As Cousin Lorenzo and his wife Gianina showed me to my third-floor room they made me feel very welcome and assured me that Papa would soon come to visit. For the first time in my life, I felt wanted—and I had a room to myself.

Lorenzo and Gianina had no children, and the way they treated me gave me the sense that I was filling a void in their lives. This might have been a little hard on the niece and nephew who lived in this extended family, as affection now was spread among three children. However, it was wonderful for me.

Every morning *Comare* Serafina milked the goats, and I was awakened to a breakfast of fresh goat milk and bread. And every morning, I would help Cousin Lorenzo clean his stable of thirty draft horses before he went off to his job as construction contractor. There were barnyard chickens, geese, and ducks as well as the large herd of goats who were all in the care of *Comare* Serafina. Nobody else touched or fed these animals.

On Saturdays I occasionally went out and drove a one-horse roller and compacted the cinder-paved streets that Cousin LaPoppola was building. This made me feel very important because I drove the horse by myself. I was actually accomplishing something, and Cousin Lorenzo trusted me enough to do this without supervision. For the first time in my life, I felt accepted and loved by a family. I was never *made* to do anything but did everything of my own volition. I *wanted* to clean the stable, I *wanted* to drive the roller, and the freedom of choice was a heady experience. Because they trusted me, I began to realize a sense of being in charge of my own life and destiny.

Even though I was a little embarrassed to ride in Lorenzo's horse-drawn buggy because most people of Lorenzo's position drove cars, I was also proud to live with him and to be known as his helper. One Saturday afternoon, he asked me to go with him to collect some money. On the way home, we stopped at a live chicken market and bought a beautiful big goose. I held the bird and felt a little more conspicuous than usual riding along in the buggy holding this feathered spectacle in my lap. I asked Lorenzo why he hadn't bought a car.

"I did buy a Dodge touring car a couple of years ago, Johnny, but it didn't work."

"Didn't work! What do you mean?"

"Well, I thought driving a car would be like driving a horse, but on my way home from the garage the very day I bought it, I found out that is not so. That car drove itself right up onto a telephone pole guy wire and rolled over. I walked home and never went back after it. From now on, Johnny, it's just me and horses. Cars are killers as far as I'm concerned."

As I pondered Lorenzo's story of his first and last driving experience, he lit up a Guinea Stinker cigar, and I noticed my leg was getting very warm. The goose had unloaded a great shit all over my lap, and I felt more conspicuous than ever driving along in a horse and buggy, imagining everyone we passed on the sidewalk was looking at me.

Summertime was glorious. Once school was out, I could do what I liked. Two kids I had become acquainted with were helping their father bundle radishes and dandelions in his truck garden. I watched for a time and decided to help them. Every summer their father, Donato, employed a man who came from Italy to help with the garden, and the five of us worked filling the crates with fresh-washed greens. It was pleasant work, and I enjoyed it even though I had no thought of getting paid. At the end of the season, however, Donato sent for me on a Sunday morning, gave me four half-dollars, and his boys took me to a Hoot Gibson movie at Sheepshead Bay.

Living at LaPoppola's was the best year of my growing up: there was a loving family, plenty of food, a warm clean bed, and Cousin Lorenzo even gave me nickles from time to time. One of these nickles caused me to be the subject of a beating on my way to school. About fifteen schoolboys came toward me and one asked for my money.

"I don't have any," I lied when I realized I was going to be robbed. One kid kneeled behind me while another shoved me over flat on my back. Each boy had a job to do and some grabbed my flailing knees and legs while others rifled through my pockets. I was helpless, of course, and lost my precious nickle. The rest kicked me wherever they could kick me, admonishing me not to tell anyone. I told the teacher, however, but nothing was ever done about it. In spite of little incidents of this nature, I was sad when Papa showed up one day and announced he was taking me to live with him and Mike in the flat he had just rented above a grocery store. And my new-found family was sad, too, because I seemed to make up for the son they never had.

I Become Johnny Bananas

The depression had really set in, and it was impossible for an uneducated man like Papa to get work. He bought a pushcart and began selling bananas on the streets, and that is how Mike became "Bananas" and I became "Little Bananas." We would all go to the banana auction at the waterfront, and Papa would buy seventy-five or a hundred stalks which he would pay a teamster to deliver to his banana cellar in Brooklyn. The wino who helped load the wagon would ride along with the bananas and assist with the unloading. Once the green stalks were all hung from hooks in a cellar under the butcher shop, Papa lit gas heaters to help speed up the ripening process.

Business was going pretty good, so Papa decided to expand. He was selling bananas from his pushcart, and when I wasn't in school, I sold them from a small stand in front of the butcher shop. Mike talked Papa into buying an old converted taxicab that had a big box on the back end, so Mike could drive around the city selling bananas wholesale to stores. At that time Mike and Papa must have been very naive to think that they could buck the syndicate by supplying bananas to fruit retailers.

Nevertheless, with these expansionist ideas in mind, Papa bought not one but two loads of bananas, about three hundred stalks! We were exhausted when, at last, they were all hung from the ceiling of the cellar, and as soon as Papa lit the gas heaters we closed the doors on our expected fortune and went back to the flat to wait for them to ripen. Well, Mike didn't go back with us as he and a couple of friends decided to joy ride around the city. Papa and I ate peppers and bread for supper and fell asleep that night with visions of our upcoming wealth pouring in and out of our dreams.

But, as sometimes happens in New York in late spring, the weather turned very hot overnight and continued for a couple of days. By the time Papa checked on his bananas, it was too late. Opening the cellar door he was greeted by fruit that was already over-ripe. No matter that he turned off the gas immediately—the ripening process had begun and could not be stopped.

Mike was nowhere to be found, and Papa and I couldn't possibly sell bananas fast enough to secure our investment. Two days later, as the sickeningly sweet smell of rotten bananas wafted up out of our storage cellar and into our neighborhood, Papa and I realized we were financially ruined. To add insult to injury, Papa had to borrow money to pay to have the spoiled fruit hauled away.

Occasionally after that, Papa would be able to talk a wholesaler into financing a cartfull of bananas, but his credit was slipping away, and we were having a hard time getting enough money for one meal a day. And though the banana business was gone, my nickname stuck and to some old friends I am still known as "Johnny Bananas."

A Picture of Benito Mussolini and Our Italian Roots

"Il Duce is a *bravo* man," Papa announced, indicating the rotogravure picture on the wall of the kitchen as he pushed his chair back from our Easter table. The day before Papa had been to his friend, Gervasi, who did bootleg barbering at home on weekends, so he was clean shaven except for his small handle-bar mustache. He was always proud of his white teeth, so strong he could remove a beer bottle cap with them and grind them in anger so fiercely they could be heard fifteen feet away.

We had eaten our holy day meal alone—Mike never ate at the flat anymore—and though our feast had just been fried potatoes and bread there was a little more food than usual and someone had given Papa a bottle of red wine. Perhaps it was the wine that made him talkative.

"What did Mussolini do, Papa," I asked, gratefully accepting the glass of wine he proffered as I gazed at the uniformed and be-medaled picture of the man who wore a hat with tassels.

"Mussolini is Italian, Giovanni." Since Papa could not read or write in any language, his knowledge of politics amounted to scraps of information he heard on the streets from his illiterate friends. It was enough for Papa that Mussolini's picture had appeared in an American paper and that he was an Italian to make him a hero.

"There are three great men in history, Giovanni," Papa continued his lesson. "Mussolini, Giuseppi Garibaldi and King Victor Emmanuel."

The wine made me deliciously warm, and I enjoyed lingering at the table with Papa. I put my foot up on Mike's empty chair to rest my knee, which had been hurt in a cart ride down a steep hill. Leaning back, I listened to Papa and continued to sip wine as the pain in my leg grew more and more vague and Papa continued to talk, now telling stories about "the old country."

In those days the "old country" was nothing but a vague and distant place that immigrant Italians spoke about. Papa never showed it to me on a map, of course, because he could not read a map. It was forty years later that I visited my parents' village of Genzano, which is about 125 miles inland from Naples. Located atop one of the mountains in the Matese Range, Genzano is a fortress-like village of white stone buildings and cobblestone streets. Long strings of red peppers and window boxes of colorful geraniums brighten the balconies of the otherwise somber buildings. From the village I could look out across the valley and fields where Mama and Papa had worked so hard in the hot Italian sun. Also visible beyond the fields were the black mouths of caves part-way up the rock wall opposite. It must have been these caves that Papa talked about that afternoon.

"We lived in a cave outside Genzano, Giovanni—my mama, my papa, my three sisters and I. It was a fine limestone cave overlooking the fertile valley below. Every day at dawn Papa led us down the cobblestone path to the garden plots where we worked and grazed the burros and goats. I was the official goat-herder and made sure those animals browsed the hillsides and kept out of the vegetables."

"What did you grow, Papa?" Now in a slightly drunken state, I was especially happy to have Papa pay so much attention to me.

"Well, we grew zucchini, onions, spicy herbs, and many kinds of greens. I can still smell it, Giovanni—especially the plots of basil that filled the fresh Italian air with their fragrance on hot days. And the lemon trees—the sweet white blossoms, I will never forget. And at the end of the day we turned up the steep path with a basket of greens for supper.

"Sometimes Mama would make *fritatta* out of zucchini blossoms stuffed with onions and basil. There would be a great salad of every kind of greens: dandelions, endive, fennel, and lettuce all dressed with olive oil and vinegar and fresh basil. And then fresh-baked bread from our own brick oven. And often in the evening we gathered outside with our neighbors to visit before bedtime. Nearly always someone played the concertina or mandolin, and there was singing to go with a glass of wine. It was a good life, Giovanni, my boy—until all of us children began marrying."

"How did you meet my mama?"

"Our marriage was arranged when I was only two years old. It was the day of your mama Rosina's baptism, two days after her birth. Your Mama's family lived in the cave next to ours, and, of course, we joined in the baptismal celebration. My papa and her papa decided that very day that I, Vittorio Torccio, should marry Rosina Caraciano when we were old enough."

"So you grew up with Mama?" I inquired continuing to drink the wine that Papa kept pouring.

"No, because a year later the Caracianos loaded their children and their belongings on a two-wheeled cart drawn by their burro and set out for Potenza some fifty miles west. Potenza was larger and Papa Caraciano thought it held out hopes for a better life." Papa leaned back in his chair, watching the pictures that formed in his mind as he spoke.

"And then what, Papa?"

"Times became very hard when my three sisters married and their husbands came to live with us in our cave dwelling. Our small plot of land could not support all of us, especially after each of my sisters had a child. By then we were receiving letters from Cousin LaPoppola in America urging us to come, because things were much better in the new country."

"What happened next, Papa," I asked as much out of desire to keep Papa talking to me as out of interest.

Papa poured us each a little more wine and sat quietly looking into his glass for a minute. "Next. Next, we tried to make a go of it, but at last my three brothers-in-law decided to go to America and leave their wives and children with us until they could send for them. By the time the men wrote from America sending for their families, our Mama and Papa had died, and now my sisters had to think what to do with me."

The rest of the story unfolded with the waning afternoon. Papa's sisters reminded the twelve-year-old that he had been matched with Rosina at her baptism, that one day they would be married, and so he would have to go to Potenza and wait with the Caracianos until he was old enough to marry. Then the sisters wasted no time getting ready for the trip to America. They gathered their homemade Provolone, *prosciutto*, salami, bread and wine. The *carretta* was loaded, their little burro named Chico was hooked up and with four milk goats in tow, they started out for Potenza fifty miles away. Walking barefoot to save their shoes, the women each carried a bundle of belongings balanced on her head as the kids rode and slept on top of the *carretta*.

There were frequent stops to allow the goats to feed along the hilly cobblestone road. During these times, the travelers anticipating the adventure that lay ahead, ate bread and milk, but saved the dry meat and cheese for the steamship trip across the Atlantic.

"On the fourth day after leaving Genzano, Giovanni, we arrived at the Caracianos, and I saw your mama again for the first time in ten years. I was just a young boy, but I saw how beautiful she was. She was not as dark complected as most of the other girls, and she wore her light brown hair in a thick braid down her back. And your mama's eyes were as blue as the sky, Giovanni. That summer we walked along the road together gathering wild figs, but we did not speak much. We were both too shy." Papa continued talking to me and not to me. It was more as if he was telling the stories to himself by way of remembering and reliving those bitter-sweet days.

"My sisters sold Chico, their little cart and the four goats to get money for their train tickets to Naples, where they boarded the steamer. I was left behind to work as a goat-herder and grow up enough to marry your mama."

Papa and Mama married very young, and Antonio, Pasquali and Graziano were born before the letter from America arrived in 1905. A professional reader confirmed what Vittorio hoped. Cousin Lorenzo LaPoppola in New York had work for Papa in his excavating business. Lorenzo would finance the trip to America so Vito could drive a team of horses, hauling dirt in a bottom-dump wagon for the excavations.

The young couple's joy and hope were unbridled. In Italy they had been living with Rosina's parents, and the future seemed impossible and bleak. But America! America meant plenty of food, new ways of doing things, undreamed-of wealth, a house for each family, and land—so much land in the new country!

"And after I had saved enough money working for Zio Lorenzo,

I sent for your mama and the boys," Papa finished. Perhaps he did not want to recount the disappointments that had come next. The loss of work, Tony's involvement with the underworld, Mama's death, and now the impossible way we were living, dirty and half-starved most of the time. As the afternoon wore on Papa became more and more frustrated, complaining that his older sons did not support him as was expected in the old country.

Soon Papa's head fell forward, and he began snoring in his chair. My head began to spin, and I was wretching by the time I limped to the toilet. I lost the wine that had been a symbol of comradeship between Papa and me that Easter day, but I never lost the memory of the stories he told.

Lung Soup for Supper

Papa was gone from the flat every morning before I wakened. I never understood where he went because he didn't tell me, and he didn't seem to have any work. Anyway, he rarely brought home money or food, so it fell to me at age twelve to support us.

Weekdays, of course, there was school. I knew what time to leave by checking the big clock that I could see through the store window downstairs. Breakfast was no problem because I had none, and lunch was the same. Mid-morning at school most of the kids bought a bottle of milk, and I longed to have one, too but I just accepted the fact that there was none for me.

No one at school seemed to notice that I was starving. Maybe they noticed I was filthy and probably smelled unpleasant and wanted to get me out of the classroom for a while, or maybe they felt I was reliable, I don't know, but for some reason I was always chosen to run errands for the teachers. Most days I was sent out for the teachers' lunches, often spicy, hot Oriental food that nearly killed me with desire to eat. Sometimes, I was sent to Manhattan to an old abandoned school to pick up supplies. I would be given a note so the truant officer wouldn't question me, and there was always a little time to watch the firemen at the training building on 62nd Street. They would scale the side of the building with a ladder, and when they got six or eight stories high, they would jump off into the permanent net stretched between steel columns far below. I was also sent to teachers' homes with notes because many of them did not have telephones, and, sometimes, I went to the theater district to pick up tickets.

Christmas was coming and we were asked to bring canned goods to school for the needy. Of course, I couldn't bring goods, but the teacher asked me to help assemble the Christmas boxes. There was probably no "needier" family than ours, but I didn't know how to express our dire poverty, so I willingly did my job. I was pretty blue when I left the room piled high with food that day. It seemed that someone should have recognized by the skinny looks of me that I was hungry most of the time.

Several days later when I returned home from school, however, it appeared there might be a Christmas for us after all. My eyes nearly popped out of my head when at the foot of my bed—a bare springs with newspapers and a blanket—I saw a large pile of neatly wrapped Christmas presents.

"Maybe brother Pat sent us a bunch of gifts," I thought. I knew better than to touch them and sat down to wait for Mike, knowing he must have something to do with this surprise bonanza. When he arrived at last, he told me that one of his friends who had been hired for the temporary rush at the post office had stolen these boxes, and Mike had agreed to store them for him. My hopes for a Christmas were dashed again.

To make matters worse, we could no longer pay our rent. However, when our landlord went to court to get a dispossession notice, the judge sent someone to investigate. People were being turned out on the streets all over New York for failure to pay rent, and the court was beginning to recognize that this was not good. We were fortunate to get a twenty-five dollar rent voucher that allowed us to stay in our flat—even though we still had to somehow scrounge up five dollars more on our own.

It was then I went to work for Pete Suzzi, the butcher whose shop was above our defunct banana cellar. He agreed that I could deliver orders five mornings a week and all day Saturday for two dollars.

"Can you ride a bike, Johnny Bananas?" he asked the first day.

"Sure, I can," I lied. I'd never tried—but I might be able to.

"There's the bike and here is your pouch of change money. Now load these packages in the basket and get on your way."

I did as I was told, but instead of mounting the bike in front of the store, I wheeled it around the corner out of sight. The bike was on the street and I remained on the curb, knowing that it would be easier for me to mount this way. But when I did get on the bike, there was a new dilemma. I couldn't reach the pedals. Fortunately for my job, I had seen kids riding big bicycles by placing their right leg

69

through the frame, and when I did that I was surprised that I could pump the bike easier than I imagined. So, off I went on my first assignment delivering packages of meat all around the neighborhood. The job was a good one and sometimes Mr. Suzzi even shared with me the pan of pasta that his wife brought directly from the stove to the shop.

On my first payday, I bought a large beef lung from Mr. Suzzi for five cents. In order for the lung to remain looking palatable, a knot had been tied in the windpipe to keep it from collapsing. Mr. Suzzi didn't bother wrapping it for me, of course, and I very proudly carried my first purchase down the street looking forward to surprising Papa with soup for supper. On my way home I stopped at the vegetable market and asked Cheech for three cents' worth of soup greens. Cheech was glad to get anything for the half-spoiled trimmings that no one else would buy, and he even threw in some badly bruised tomatoes and soft sprouted onions. I picked up a three-cent loaf of bread and headed for the flat with my big lung getting even larger as it continued to inflate in the heat of the afternoon.

To cook supper, I first had to put a quarter in the gas meter which was located in a dark and dingy basement. Back in the apartment, I cut-up the lung and windpipe, being careful not to waste a bit of the precious food. By the time Papa returned home, the very large kettle of lung soup was bubbling on the stove. Papa, who had a keen nose for seasoned food, walked over to the simmering pot, inhaled the aroma, and instead of complimenting me, complained that the soup needed more salt. How I longed for praise that night because I was very proud of myself—but I never got it. It bothered me a lot because I was the youngest one and the only one working. The least Papa could do was appreciate me and my lung soup. Nevertheless, supper was a feast, with food left over for the next day if it didn't spoil in the heat.

Pete Suzzi soon decided to move his shop across the street, where, for some unknown reason, he went broke. That ended my delivery job.

Fired From My Next Job

I began coughing at night and Papa sometimes gave me *grappa*, a brandy made from grape squeezings. I soon found a small bottle which I filled with this cough medicine and carried to school with me, the teacher never suspecting I was drinking brandy. One day, however, when I had had nothing to eat for two days but some fruit I managed to steal while helping to unload a shipment of wine grapes, I must have passed out in school. When I came to, I found myself in Coney Island Hospital, where they were going to keep me overnight until the city health doctor diagnosed me.

It turned out I had acute diphtheria and small wonder. Our flat was infested with roaches and bedbugs, and recently—checking under the bathtub for the source of a terrible smell—I had found a dead sewer rat. Papa and Mike inquired at school when I did not return home at all that night, and the next day Mike came on foot and walked me, still wobbly and sick, back home.

Shortly after this the grocer downstairs offered to give me free milk if I would come for it once a day. It was bulk milk, and I brought the only kettle that we had, a large pot for boiling pasta. He slipped a one-pint dipper into his large 10-gallon can and poured the milk which was barely enough to cover the bottom of my big container. But I was very grateful, because, now, Papa and I could have bread and milk for supper.

I also felt pretty lucky to find a bike near the curb of a deserted street in Manhattan Beach where all the rich people lived. No matter that it had no tires and made a terrible racket as I rode away with it. I was never sure whether the owner was angry or happy that someone took his delapidated velocipede.

When I was thirteen, I got a job from the Strauss butcher chain and earned four dollars a week. I had to give the money to Papa, of course, but I wanted to keep some for myself. For ten cents I could go to the Hot Dog Show at Coney Island. This was a large smoke-filled room with round tables and bentwood chairs that was open twenty-four hours a day, and the dime admission allowed the customers the choice of a hot dog or a piece of pie with coffee as well as being able to watch the movie.

On one occasion I held out twenty-five cents from my wages because I had made up my mind to go to Coney Island. I was pretty strong so Papa couldn't force me to give it to him, but the struggle was so unpleasant that after that I stole my money back from him while he was sleeping. He would put his change on the chair beside his bed and after he was snoring loudly, I would take eleven or twelve cents, and Papa never suspected because he couldn't count very well. No wonder he went broke in the banana business, unexpected hot weather or not.

Just when things were going a little better for me because of my

71

job, I lost it. One Saturday night about nine o'clock a well-dressed man came up to me as I was washing the white enameled meat trays.

"How old are you?" he asked politely.

"Thirteen," I answered eagerly, proud to have such a job at my age.

"And when did you start work today?"

"I come in at eight o'clock every Saturday and work until nine. On school days I can't get here until one o'clock," I said, volunteering even more than I was asked.

The nice man thanked me, went up front to the manager, presented him with a summons, and I was fired on the spot because I was too young. What did age have to do with it, I wondered, if my boss was satisfied with my work. Here I was willing to work, but society wouldn't permit me to. This must be the reason people started stealing.

The Last Days of School

The picture was of a small sick-looking dog walking up the sidewalk toward the door of a big building labeled The American Society for the Prevention of Cruelty for Animals. I had drawn it, and it won a prize, the only prize I ever won at school. I suppose it was my way of expressing the anguish I felt at the beating brother Pat had given me. It hung for a while in the Metropolitan Museum of Art in a collection of school drawings.

Papa was panhandling and borrowing from friends, and he thought if he could just get his citizenship papers that he might be able to find work. For a fee of fifteen dollars there were people who would make arrangements with the right officials to get him his papers. It wouldn't matter whether he could read or write; they would fix it up. He eventually saved enough money to do it, but he never got his final papers.

When eighth-grade graduation was coming up, I asked the teacher ahead of time if I was going to graduate because I would need to scrounge a pair of pants for the occasion. My shoes would do because the tops were pretty good—though I had to carry folded newspaper in my pockets and replace it in the soles several times a day to cover the holes. My teacher looked thoughtful, rather reluctant, and finally said I would graduate. Maybe I really didn't qualify.

Brother Mike really came through for me. He bought me a new

pair of pants and an autograph album. My friends signed the book addressing me as either Johnny Bananas or Louie Ricarno, the name of the actor who played Capone in the movie. In the space after "My hero" I wrote Al 'Scarface' Capone.

Graduation night arrived, and again no member of my family was present. As I walked up to receive the district diploma, no one applauded. Then, suddenly, a lone person who maybe felt sorry for me gave a couple of claps.

5

The Depression Deepens

We Run Away and Return

Since Moishe, Charlie and I were all a little heady with importance at having graduated from elementary school, we decided to strike out on our own. Kids who wanted to run away in those days went down to Greenwich Market and helped the drivers load their trucks in exchange for a ride out of New York City. We arrived early in the morning, loaded the truck with empty wooden boxes and got a ride to western Pennsylvania.

There was no work to be had except the odd job that got us a meal, so we lived by our wits stealing milk from doorsteps to keep us going. Sometimes we were able to take pastries from small Ma and Pa stores, but we were getting desperate by the time we reached central Pennsylvania. Then, late one afternoon as we walked along a country lane, we came upon two men speaking broken English.

"Do you have any work for us?" I asked speaking for the others as well as myself even though I was the youngest.

"You kids from the city?" the man with the Italian accent asked. "Things getting worse and worse in the city. We got no money either, but we got food," he went on, and I felt a wave of relief wash through me because I was pretty sure we would get work here.

The Italian said I could go home with him, and the other man, a Pole, took Charlie because his parents were from Poland. Moishe was left, but the two farmers knew an Irish family that was childless, and they agreed to keep Moishe. There was to be no money for our work—just board and room—but we were grateful as we climbed aboard the horse drawn wagon.

I hoed spuds and learned to milk cows, feeling productive and contented. But not so Charlie and Moishe. Perhaps their homes in Brooklyn were better than mine; soon they came to me complaining they were homesick. With the optimism of children in our hearts, we set off early one morning, headed back to New York. My Italian boss gave us a fruit jar full of milk, and we arrived hungry and tired at the Philadelphia market by eight o'clock that evening. Since there were no rides available, we spent the night walking and hitching, stealing milk from doorsteps as we went. Afraid to be caught by the police, we gorged ourselves with milk and left the unfinished bottles on the curb.

The rides were scarce, so we waited at a stoplight and climbed on the open tailgate of a large van where there was just enough room for us to stand holding on to the ropes that secured the cargo. Because we had not slept, we took turns keeping each other awake. Finally, a car pulled up to the cab of the truck and warned the driver who chased us off. When we arrived at last in Brooklyn, Moishe's mother wanted to have me arrested for leading the other two kids astray. Papa, on the other hand, had not been at all concerned with my disappearance.

Odd Jobs and A Little About Sex

There was still the summer to be gotten through before starting high school, and I went to work for Toni Monti's brother-in-law, Bill, scrapping old cars for a sandwich a day. One of my first jobs was dismantling an almost new Chrysler that Bill's detective friend had arranged to have Bill steal, so the detective could collect the insurance. Toni and I worked in an old shed quickly taking out the engine, which Bill sold to the rum runners along with the wheels and tires. Because those old cars had a lot of wood in them, it was relatively easy for Toni and me to winch the body into the empty lot next door and set it afire. By the time two detectives arrived on the scene, there wasn't a trace of the Chrysler.

As the depression deepened, the unemployment lines grew longer and longer. Once a week that summer I went to Manhattan and joined lines of men waiting for work, but the older men were chosen over me. Bill, however, put Toni and me to work for a short time digging a basement under a building at Brighton Beach, for a dollar a day. But my most interesting job that summer was hauling ashes out of the basement of a house of prostitution.

We got the job from Ibrahim, a barker at an exotic dancer side-show in Coney Island, who lived nearby. He was a very dark Turk with tattooed temples and hands whose stories about jumping ship when he was with the Turkish Navy fascinated me. Ibrahim was over eighty and his deeply wrinkled face was accentuated by his toothless grin. Most of the time he wore no hat to cover his shiny bald pate, but when he went to work he wore a white turban on his head, bright red Turkish pantaloons and a satin shirt.

In addition to being a barker, Ibrahim was landlord for several of the girls from the sideshow who used his rooms for prostitution. Toni and I worked hard all morning, hauling several years' accumulation of cinders up the basement steps to the alley. About noon one of the girls appeared with a pitcher of homebrew, and much to our amazement she was wearing nothing but a long black veil with only a G-string underneath. I had never seen a woman's bare breasts before except when she was nursing, and for some reason this didn't look the same to me. She left us with the pitcher of beer and considerable concern over her scanty clothes.

"Johnny, did you see her tits through that veil?" fifteen-year-old Toni exclaimed.

"Boy, did I. And were they big!" I enthused. "How would you like to nuzzle them?"

"I wonder how much whores charge."

"Two dollars," I demonstrated my worldly knowledge. "All whores charge two dollars."

Toni looked away dreamily and asked, "I wonder if a guy could buy a dollar's worth." He was undoubtedly considering how to spend his hard-earned buck.

"Have you every screwed a woman?"

"Never a whore," he answered, inferring that he had screwed other women.

"Don't try to 'shit' me. The only 'woman' that you ever screwed was 'lady five fingers'."

"Ah, bullshit. You jerk-off, too." Masturbation was supposed to lead to insanity.

"I know what I'm gonna do with *my* buck," I went on. "They're having a hot dog and hamburger war in Coney Island, and they cost three cents each. And I'm going down and buy a big stack of them." At fourteen I still preferred food to sex, but that was to change.

Advised to Quit School and Another Beating

September came, and I started the ninth grade at the Abraham Lincoln High School annex. I was still just as hungry and dirty as I had been in grade school and, to add to my unhappiness, the teacher told me to bring soap and a towel for gym class. But we had no soap, and the only towel we had at home was a cotton cement sack which we used for all purposes, so I was unable to comply. Nevertheless, after gym, we were all herded into a large shower room where the custodian controlled the water temperature. When he felt we had enough hot water, he would turn it to icy cold and there would be pandemonium because we could not escape it until he unlocked the door to let us out. To further add to my misery, I had to pull my dirty clothes onto my shivering wet body and wait for them to dry during the next class.

There was another problem during these first few days of school. I had three abscessed teeth that hurt constantly, and as I sat in class I kept one finger in my mouth most of the time, trying to loosen one or the other of the teeth. Pushing and pulling caused the abscess to break and ease the pain, and after many hours, one tooth yielded. This encouraged me to keep on until after two days, I pushed one out. This felt so good that I continued the same treatment on the other two and had all three of them out in another week.

About a month had gone by when Miss Goetches, my elderly biology teacher, asked me to stay after school to explain my drawing of an onion cell. Looking back, it seems ironical that I was expected to replicate frog and onion cells when I would have been much happier having these items home for my supper. At the time I did not question it, of course, and defended my work as I felt I had done the assignment rather well. Miss Goetches had other thoughts.

"Johnny, I think you should quit school," she said flat out.

"Can I really do that?" I asked, excited at the possibility.

"Yes. You've finished the eighth grade, you're fourteen years old, and you can get your working papers."

My head was swimming with the joyous thought that I was educated—finished with school. Now, I could just go out into the adult world and work. My elation continued even though Mike and Papa showed no enthusiasm for my new-found place in the universe. Perhaps they knew that since they couldn't find work, there was little chance for me whether I had my working papers or not.

And they were right: though I looked for work, I couldn't find it and had to go back to wrecking cars for Bill for the same meager midday sandwich. I was out in the lot cutting up old chassis with a hammer and chisel late one afternoon when Papa appeared on the scene and ordered me to get home. I could see from the look on his face that he was furious, and I dropped my tools in the dirt and started for the flat with Papa close behind me muttering cuss words in Italian.

"What's wrong, Papa?" I asked as we flew up the stairs.

"Why didn't you cook supper?" he shouted, grinding his teeth as he always did when he was angry.

"You didn't leave me any money, Papa," I defended myself.

"When I got up this morning, I went to your bed and told you to get fifteen cents' credit at the butcher shop, but you did not obey your Papa."

I started to tell him that I had no memory of that when he began kicking and punching me, becoming more insane with rage as he continued to attack. I could not hit back at my papa, of course, so I turned and flew down the stairs scarcely touching a step as I went. I stopped at the doorway to the street, hoping that it was over when Papa called down to me.

"Get back up here," he shouted in Italian.

"Are you through beating me, Papa?" I inquired.

"Get back up here," he shouted again, and because I believed that he must be over his rabid insanity, I obediently climbed back up the stairs. The minute I got to the kitchen, he slapped me a couple of times, went over to the drainboard and, picking up a butcher knife, came towards me. At this point I decided to leave in a hurry and sailed down the stairs knowing I would never sleep under my Papa's roof again, as I was sure he was capable of killing me.

Frightened that Papa might follow, I sneaked on the subway and, once more, left New York by hitching a ride on a truck out of Greenwich Market. I was only to see Papa once again in my lifetime. About a year later, I noticed him approaching down the street and turned up a side street to avoid him. Surely, his inability to find work and his bad luck had driven him half-mad. Also, because Mama had done all disciplining, perhaps he knew no other way to handle what appeared to him to be my disobedience. Whatever it was, I went on to new adventures, hearing many years later that Papa had died alone and unhappy.

Aimless Wandering

I was hitchhiking in West Virginia, getting more and more desperate for work and food. No matter which direction I was going, it always appeared there was more traffic going the opposite way, and since I had no particular destination, I often crossed the road and started thumbing the other way when a car came along. At last a farmer picked me up and dropped me off near a farmhouse where my hunger pangs encouraged me to knock on the door and ask for help.

A kindly-looking woman with shoulder-length gray hair appeared and asked what I wanted. She was nicely attired in a clean house dress and apron, and I felt nervous but hopeful.

"Ma'am, do you have some work for me to do in exchange for a sandwich? Any kind of work," I pleaded. "I'll do anything."

"No!" The kindliness I thought I had seen in her face disappearing as she frowned down at me.

"Do you have any bread or food that you are going to throw away. I don't care what it is," I begged quickly before she could say more.

"No! And get off my property immediately." She slammed the door in my face.

As I walked down the lane toward the highway, bitter tears came to my eyes, not so much because she wouldn't give me the food but because she wouldn't let me work for it. A terrible anger welled up in me, and without considering the ramifications, I felt that if I had a gun I would use it if it would help me get food.

By now I was so hopeless that I decided to go back to Suffern to see if the climate had changed with brother Pat. Several years had passed and I thought he might have mellowed and could possibly help me find work. I arrived late at night and seeing no lights, I slept on the floor in the hallway until they awakened in the morning.

There I was again—the phantom kid always showing up unannounced. They were very surprised, but they didn't show any anger.

"I quit school and am looking for work," I hastened to explain lest they might think I was just moving in on them.

During breakfast I told Pat that Papa had beaten me and let it go at that. I did not say he had tried to kill me. Pat explained that there was little work around Suffern, but I could iron shirts at his laundry in return for board and room. He went on to say that Angie was coming out of the orphanage to live with them in a month, and that I would have to leave at that time. At least, I had a month's reprieve before I would be homeless again.

At the laundry I met one of the chief executives of the California Perfume Company, the predecessor to Avon. I asked Mr. Williams if there was work at his factory, and he told me to report to his secretary. Mr. Williams had been very encouraging, and I felt confident that I would get a job. The interview was going just fine

79

until the question of my age came up.

"I am fourteen," I answered very proudly, "and I have working papers."

"You are too young and cannot work in this plant," the secretary said with finality.

At that moment I decided to add more years to my age and suddenly became eighteen.

It was the end of my month with Pat, and Angie was due in a couple of days, so I was on the road again. After hitching back to Brooklyn, I found myself in Prospect Park preparing to spend the night on a bench. I knew I would never go back to Papa, and Cousin Lorenzo came to mind. But for some reason I felt that I was too far from that part of the family to impose myself on them. The only one I could turn to, I felt, was brother Tony.

The Blue Dye in My Socks Causes Gangrene

Arriving at Tony's the next day, I was made to feel welcome even though he already had his in-laws living with him. Tony said I could sleep on the sunporch, and that first night as I sat on the edge of my wicker couch bed pulling off my socks, I felt an urgent itching in my right big toe. On closer examination I found a large open blister discolored by the blue dye of the ten-cent pair of socks. During the past two months and my travels on foot, my socks had never been washed and had caked to my feet. I had been too concerned with other matters to be aware of the condition of my disintegrating footwear, but now I was forced to pay attention to my swelling leg.

All night long an uncontrollable itching continued—moving from my foot up my leg, it reached beyond my knee by morning. At daylight I saw that my leg was not only swollen but discolored as well, and when I tried to bend my knee, I couldn't because the skin was stretched so tight. Now, the pain was beginning, and I knew I was in trouble. Minnie, Tony's second wife—or she might have been his third—told me to go to Coney Island Hospital which was about a mile away. With no cane, no crutch, I hobbled and hopped dragging my sick leg along the best I could. In the receiving room, I joined about seventy-five people, mostly pregnant women, waiting their turn.

When I finally got to an examining room, the two young interns took one look at me and decided something had to be done immediately.

"It looks like gangrene to me," the first young doctor said.

Even though I didn't know exactly what "gangrene" meant it scared the shit out of me; I had heard of so many soldiers in World War I dying of gangrene. At this point the doctor directed a nurse to bring him an instrument, and when she appeared with something that looked more like a carpenter's twenty-penny spike, I thought it was truly an instrument of torture.

What happened next is a study in human endurance and approach-avoidance conflict. Without benefit of anesthetic, the doctor took the shiny spike and pushed it through the all-but-bursting skin of my ankle, the resultant pain so excruciating that I almost blacked out. The suffering was partially compensated, however, by the encircling arms of the two nurses who held and comforted me. As the doctor continued to pierce my foot pushing the instrument in until the point came out on the opposite side, the nurses squeezed tighter and reassured me that everything would be all right. Their mothering was something I had had little of in my life, and I wanted it to continue, but at last when I could bear the pain no longer I cried for the doctor to stop.

After a few more punctures, the doctor quit. When I looked down at my foot expecting to see blood oozing, I was surprised to find my foot and leg completely dry.

"You must go home, now, and soak your foot in very hot water with Epsom salts. Soak it for twenty minutes and remove it for twenty minutes all night long. And tomorrow, bring in a legal guardian to sign so we can amputate your leg," he said rather casually.

My pain was so bad at this point that I could scarcely comprehend his words. The two nurses looked sympathetic as they left the room and came back with a cane to help me make the trip home.

"I don't have a legal guardian," I whispered feebly.

"Bring somebody," the doctor ordered curtly.

As I limped home the pain and the impending amputation made me realize why Coney Island Hospital was dubbed "the butcher shop." The thought of losing my leg was overwhelming, but at the same time I felt it was better than dying from gangrene. Stumbling homeward, I envisioned myself with a crutch and peg leg like the many war amputees in Brooklyn at that time.

My pain and depression were devastating as I eased my nearly-exploding foot into the tub of hot water and salts. I could not sit because my leg was so swollen that my knee would not bend.

Watching the clock move torturously slowly, I wondered what good this treatment could possibly do for me. Twenty minutes in the steaming water and twenty minutes out. About five minutes into the second bath, pus began oozing out of the punctures that the intern had made in my foot. I couldn't believe my eyes: the yellowish-green drainage solidified in the hot water turning into long wormlike creatures that writhed as though they were alive. What made this horrible vision bearable was that the pain began to subside, and I knew that if I continued the regimen during the night, I would probably be all right by morning and my leg would not have to be amputated.

Looking For Work, Gloria Lifts Her Dress, and Sex with an Older Woman

After my leg healed I went to Manhattan looking for work. I really didn't know how to go about getting a job, but when I saw older men standing in line, I would join them. Needless to say, the older men were always hired over me—an inexperienced fourteen-year-old kid claiming to be eighteen.

I knew there were soup lines on the waterfront near the Fulton Fish Market, so I made sure I got down there about noon. The homeless and jobless milled around cooking hobo stew in milk cans bubbling away over fires made of produce crates.

"What do I have to do to get some soup?" I inquired of one grimy chef.

"Do you see that garbage scow tied over there, kid?" he asked. "Go find yourself a can and wash it in one of the fish markets and come back."

When I returned with my relatively-clean tomato can, he asked if I had brought anything for the pot. At that point, a horse-drawn wagon loaded with celery was passing by; I reached into a crate and pulled out a head as my contribution. The cook chopped it up immediately, adding it to the boiling pot.

Though I was almost constantly looking for work, I was still just a kid, too. Sometimes a group of us played dice on the street in Gerrard Court, a short block of white stucco bungalows separating Sheepshead Bay Creek from Banner Avenue. Gloria Koan lived in the court with her attractive divorced mother, whose beauty often caused evil thoughts to run through our minds. It was not lost on us, even though we were young, that thirteen-year-old Gloria was going to follow in her mother's footsteps as a classic Jewish beauty. We were in no way prepared, however, for what was to happen one warm summer evening.

Irish Flicker, who always carried a pair of dice, had organized a group of us to shoot craps for pennies. We were only vaguely aware during the game that Gloria was watching us from her porch steps. The game broke up, and we stood in a circle discussing what we would do for the rest of the evening, when Gloria squeezed in between Moishe and me. There she stood, not saying a word as we gaped at her long dark curls and her young breasts just beginning to show under the light summer dress. To our utter surprise and amazement, Gloria suddenly lifted her skirt up to her belly button revealing the fact that she had no pants. "Look!" she exclaimed proudly pointing at her crotch, "I'm grown up now. See, I have hair."

We riveted our eyes to Gloria's pubic area with its new crop of hair, all of us too stunned to utter a word. It must have dawned on each of us at the about the same time that we would be jail bait if anyone came upon the scene, and we all struck out in different directions, leaving Gloria standing with her dress still raised and a look of bewilderment on her face as if to say, "Did I do something wrong?"

Since I was unable to find a job by myself, Tony found work for me at his plumbing shop. It was against the rules for relatives to work together, so I was assigned to apprentice with an Irishman. We were assigned to refurbishing some old sandstone tenements in south Brooklyn. Their new owner, the wealthy Mr. Bommer, dressed very formally in an Oxford gray suit and Stetson hat. His white pointed goatee was always neatly trimmed and made him look very distinguished. Each morning he arrived in a chauffeur-driven car to watch the master plumber whom he considered an artist.

In those days, all of the houses were piped with lead, and the joints were made of molten solder. The liquid tin and lead were poured from a ladle onto the pipe and ran around and down the joint into the canvas-protected hand of the plumber, who then wiped and shaped the joint until it hardened. Each craftsman had to control the slowly sagging molten metal by spitting into the wiping pad, using his saliva to cool the bottom of the joint. If an inspector was mean, the plumber could get even by not cooling the joint properly and allowing a needle point to hang down so the unsuspecting building controller would cut himself as he rubbed his hand across the bottom of the razor-sharp joint.

Mr. Bommer would stand in awe for an hour or more watching the plumber sculpt perfect elliptical shapes from the flowing metal.

"That man is truly an artist," he would remark. "People don't realize that men who do such work are really professionals."

My brother Tony was an excellent craftsman, too, and at times he was hired by someone wanting to go into the plumbing business to take the test for him. The person desiring the license would buy off the proper officials in city hall and pay Tony fifty dollars.

When my temporary helper's job ended, I found employment in a shoe factory doing tedious repetitive work. I looked forward to my first weekly paycheck, which was to be seven dollars for six days work. The paymaster brought the small yellow pay envelopes around in a shoebox, and handed me one with my name and the amount of six dollars and thirty cents written on it.

"Where's my other seventy cents?"

"Ten-percent of everybody's wages is held out for union dues. And if you don't want to pay it, you're out of work."

I had to pay five dollars a week to Tony for room and board, so I was left with sixty cents for carfare and seventy cents for clothing and entertainment. The ten percent payment to protect my job by a non-existent union galled me, and I finally quit. My next job was seven days a week for seven dollars, but I didn't have to pay the ten percent kickback money. Besides, I was working with horses at the track at Coney Island and this excited my hidden dream of being a cowboy.

Part of the job was to attract people and entice them to ride the horses. While hanging onto the pommel, I soon learned how to dismount and mount a three-quarter Indian piebald at full gallop.

When things got slow, the boss would order in his broken Italian, "Johnny, do tricks." This gave me an excuse to ride and show off to the people on the boardwalk and I soon became known as "the Coney Island Cowboy."

Not all of my job was this exciting, however. Starting early in the morning, I had to clean the stalls, wash the horses with soap and water, and currycomb them until they were ready for the track. Each boy rode a big horse and led six others along the bridle path to Coney Island. Our main job then became walking alongside, holding kids on saddles so they wouldn't be thrown off. My friend Hymie always seemed to have lots of spending money, and when I asked him "how come?" he shared the secret of his wealth.

"Johnny, you can do it too. Watch which pocket a kid puts his change in, gallup the pony, and while he is bouncing get his money. When the kid comes back complaining that he lost his change, fake looking for it in the soft sand. It's easy."

So, that was how Hymie was able to buy lots of hot dogs. And, from time to time, I had even looked for lost change for some of his victims! In spite of Hymie's wealth, I was never able to pick pockets because it never seemed right.

One day a very attractive, well-dressed woman came to the ticket booth to hire a large chestnut stallion that she had been watching from the boardwalk. She wanted to take the horse out of the track and go for a ride on the bridle path. It was finally agreed that if she came on a slow day, she could hire the horse for a couple of hours, so the next Wednesday, much to our surprise, she appeared in full riding habit—derby, riding crop, and shiny boots—carrying a bag of apples and carrots.

"Johnny, you go with her and see that she doesn't gallop or whip the horse."

As we trotted along together on Ocean Parkway, I inquired about her work because she was so well-dressed.

"I'm the society editor for the *New York Times*," she confided. "I go to lots of swanky affairs to get my news."

I didn't know what "swanky" meant but I agreed with her that

Brighton Beach, 1933

those were the places to go. After about an hour, we turned back, me lagging behind because I felt embarrassed by my crummy clothes. At the end of the ride she gave me a fifty-cent tip and thanked us profusely for letting her ride the horse.

I had another encounter with a woman that was much more intimate before the track closed for the winter in November. It was not uncommon for for us to pick up girls and give them a ride as we took the horses back to the stable in the evening. One warm summer night, Pauline was watching the horses from the sidewalk as she had many other nights after her nursing shift was over.

"Can I have a ride with you to the stable, Johnny?" she called.

"OK," I said quietly. "Meet me up the street so the boss doesn't see."

Pauline was an attractive brunette with hair bobbed in the fashion of the day, unmarried, and well-built. She wore a light cotton summer dress with flowers printed on it in shades of yellow and green.

"Hold on to the pommel real tight," I said. "I will control the horse as we go under the 'El', and just let's hope there isn't a train rumbling overhead that will make the horses bolt."

As I helped her on the horse, her dress slipped above her knees and, much to my excitement, she didn't attempt to cover herself.

"I'm exposing my thighs to the world, Johnny!" she exclaimed.

As we rode along in and out of the pools of light shining down from the standards, I could see her white flesh, and I kept remembering that she was not wearing underpants—another detail I had noted earlier while helping her mount. Continuing down the wooded path, I kept having sexual fantasies about Pauline, but quickly dismissed them because she was so much older than I. I just didn't think it was possible for this fifteen-year-old kid to get anywhere with such a mature woman. And, besides that, I had never gotten anywhere with any woman before—I had never even been close to one.

At the stable I fed and bedded down the horses. When I had finished, I found her lying seductively on a reclaimed park bench inside the exercise ring. There was a large oak tree right in the center, and the area was surrounded by a tall board fence that gave us complete seclusion. A full August moon shone overhead, and a bare bulb burned dimly just inside the stable door. As I surveyed the romantic scene, I wasn't bothered that it included a large pile of horse manure.

Looking For Work, Gloria Lifts Her Dress

I was surprised when Pauline motioned me to sit beside her. Could I believe what was happening? She drew me toward her and touched her lips to mine in a way that I had never experienced before. For a few brief moments we held each other tenderly before she began unveiling to me the mysteries of the female body. She was a nurse, a woman of the world, and I was just a wildly excited kid.

Had we been in a different place, I think we might have continued exploring the possibilities of delight for the rest of the night. But the park bench wasn't comfortable, and I didn't have the finesse to draw her into the hayloft. So, I walked her to the trolley car and casually said "So Long," as she boarded for her ride to Brighton Beach. My head and heart were not casual, however, and had I but known how, I would have begged her for another date. Instead, unable to afford a ride, I turned and began walking home.

A Little Counterfeiting, Bootlegging and Gambling

Freddie and Tom were close friends of mine, and I often went to their house. They had learned how to make a few nickles by buying punchboards and suckering kids to spend their money. Big Tom, their father, was a counterfeiter; he specialized in dollar bills, which were easier to pass in those days than bills of larger denomination. One batch, however, was badly printed and had to be destroyed. Instead of burning them in a furnace, he stupidly built a fire in an empty lot across the street. He was not even careful to see that all of the bills were completely destroyed, and the neighborhood kids gathered up the unburned bills and took them to their parents.

Inevitably, one of the parents informed the police. Big Tom was taken into custody, but his people posted bail and got him out in a hurry. Several weeks later, as he walked to the subway on his way to stand trial, he was gunned down two blocks from his house by men in a speeding car. That was the end of the family because the boys' mother was already dead. Young Tom vowed that he would avenge the killers even if it took him the rest of his life, and both boys disappeared into the underworld.

In our neighborhood, bootlegging was more prevalent than counterfeiting. Brother Tony, who was involved in both bootlegging and gambling, often brought a load of raw alcohol into the basement of our house to be stored until he distributed it to "cutters" to dilute and flavor somewhere else. This liquor was then bottled, labeled "Canadian Club" and sold to saloons.

87

One block away from our house were two huge auto storage garages where the bootleg alcohol was made. I could walk past one of these buildings, look in the waist-high windows and clearly see the fermenting mash cooking in gigantic vats. The odor from this process permeated the neighborhood, and it was so strong that it would have been impossible for the police to ignore it unless they were "being taken care of."

On Sunday afternoons, Tony ran a dice game in his basement. About twenty gamblers would arrive on foot, so there would be no tell-tale cars parked outside, and go directly to the blanket-covered table set up downstairs near the steam boiler. A large porcelain light fixture shaded the single bulb that lit the room. Tony raked twenty-five cents a pass, and Max banked the game paying Tony five dollars for the sole privilege. If there was a police raid, Tony would have to go bail for the players.

My job was to take care of the door, admitting only those who wanted to gamble. Tony's wife and child went to the matinee, so they would not be in the house while the game was going on. About two o'clock one Sunday afternoon, there was a knock on the door, and I could see two policemen through the glass.

"The cops are here!" I warned the gamblers as I took my time answering the door.

"We have a complaint of a disturbance at 1112 Banner Avenue," the first cop said.

"Our house is 1110 Banner, and the house next door is 1114, and there is no 1112 Banner," I explained. "And I have been sitting here all afternoon reading the comics, and haven't seen anything un-usual," I went on, lying.

Apparently the cops bought my story because they went on their way. When I reported to Tony, brother Mike who was also there asked if one of the cops had been Joe Espozito. Yes, one of them was Joe, and Mike convinced Tony to let him go and fix it up because Joe was a friend of his.

Mike caught up with the cops several hundred feet down the street and soon returned assuring everyone that the matter had been taken care of. But, fifteen minutes after the precinct shift change, six radio-equipped Ford roadsters arrived and surrounded the house. A dozen cops and one sergeant covered all the windows and doors twirling their night sticks. Again I warned the gamblers in the basement, and as I turned back to the door pulling open the curtain, I was eye to eye with the sergeant who pounded on the door saying,

"Open up! This is a raid!"

Tony was up the stairs standing behind me as I opened the door.

"What's going on?" he demanded. "We're just having a social dice game with a bunch of friends."

"We've got proof that you're running a gambling house here." the sergeant said.

"How much will it cost for you to forget about it?" Tony asked as he invited the sergeant and two other officers into the dining room. Tony and the sergeant sat on opposite ends of the long table as the two cops, Mike and I stood watching the procedure. The rest of the officers guarded the windows and doors to prevent any of the gamblers from escaping.

"How much is this gonna cost me?" Tony asked, knowing that he was responsible for protecting the gamblers.

"Ten dollars for each officer and twenty-five for me," the sergeant responded without so much as blinking an eye.

"Bullshit," Tony hollered. "I can bail them out of jail cheaper than that, and you know it. I ain't making that kind of money."

When the sergeant kept insisting, Tony said, "Forget it! Just take us all to jail, goddammit."

The sergeant hesitated, and Tony knew it was time to make his last offer. "Fifteen bucks for you and five bucks for each of your men. That's it! Take it or lock us up!"

The sergeant didn't take long to make up his mind, and the deal was consummated quickly with Tony shelling out seventy-five dollars on the spot and agreeing to meet with the sergeant again. As the dark green roadsters disappeared down the street and around the corner, the gamblers resumed their game in the basement confident that they would not be harassed again.

I was wide-eyed and surprised at the business-like negotiating between Tony and the law-enforcement officer. A few minutes before I had been convinced that we were all going to go to jail, but Tony saved the day with his ability to negotiate. I was learning from brother Tony, becoming educated in the ways of beating the law.

The Blue Diamond Club and the Three Cs

Brother Mike also taught me things. He had belonged to a social club composed of neighborhood men when he was single. He suggested that I and other unmarried young men in the area start a club of our own, explaining that this way we could meet girls and have

89

a place to dance that wouldn't cost us very much. About fifteen of us rented a basement in Brighton Beach for five dollars a month. We painted it blue, decorating the ceiling to look like a night sky with stars, comets, moons and planets that Mike had cabbaged onto in his work in the theatrical district of Times Square.

When we were finished with our handiwork, we called our organization The Blue Diamond Social Club. We furnished it with cast-off davenports and chairs and a record player. A few of the fellows had girlfriends and they came down and brought other girls. Word spread fast that the Blue Diamond was a good place to dance and have fun, be out of the weather, and meet boys. Within a few weeks, we were overwhelmed with women from Brighton Beach and Coney Island, and the Blue Diamond became a passion pit.

Partitioned off from the main dance floor was the furnace room, where we installed a davenport for those inclined to have sex. The furnace room soon became more popular than the dance floor, with couples waiting anxiously for their turn. It wasn't unusual for those who couldn't wait to use an overstuffed chair in a corner of the dimly lit dance floor.

I had told brother Mike about my night with Pauline, and ever since, he had kept me in rubbers. One Saturday night when he made no move to give me my usual safeties, I signaled across the room to him by miming that I was rolling something along my index finger. Mike caught on immediately, disappeared into the bedroom and returned palming the rubbers as he handed them to me.

"What are you doing?" Mike's wife asked angrily, knowing full well what he had given me.

"Nothing," Mike lied.

She started crying, "Johnny is just a kid. You men are all alike."

I was surprised at her reaction because I thought sex was OK. And not wanting to get into a family feud, I pocketed my rubbers and left.

Our favorite record that winter was Hoagy Carmichael's "Stardust," and I was enjoying the slow waltz with the luscious Clara Stein in my arms when I noticed Abie Schwartz in a dark corner. Abie and Shirley Greenfield were engaged in some heavy loving, and I became anxious for him because he was noted for premature ejaculation. This night was no different; Abie suddenly got up leaving his confused girl, and started towards me with bowed legs and a look of disgust on his face.

"Abie," I queried, "did you shit your pants?" I tried to make light of it.

"Bananas, you know goddam well what I did. I came in my drawers again," he said, close to tears. "I don't think I'll ever get into a woman."

It wasn't all sex and dancing the winter that I was sixteen, however. One Saturday night a group of Greek boys from Coney Island came to the Blue Diamond Club to avenge a fight that had started the previous summer over a simple flirtation between a girlfriend of one of the Greeks and one of our boys. It had snowed, thawed and then frozen, so by the time the Greek boys arrived there was glare ice all over the sidewalk and street.

We Blue Diamond boys answered their challenge by going into the street to fight, which was why the bloodshed we had expected never materialized. Every time one guy swung on somebody else, he fell to the ice. If two grappled in their anger, both would fall down. The whole thing became a slapstick comedy, and, at last, we all laughed and shook hands. Shaking hands was customary in those days—win or lose. We wound up with a few black eyes and bruised faces, but no one was hurt badly.

Winter continued, getting colder and colder. I was without work, and the snow that fell incessantly on the city only made me more miserable. There was little activity on the streets except a few half-frozen chestnut vendors who huddled near their fires, or the occasional brave teamster trying to control his wild-eyed horse, slipping and falling on the glaze beneath its hooves.

George Terra, known as the Georgia Terror though he had never been out of New York, was a well-known boxer in the area. The precinct committeeman gave him ten work tickets to distribute to his friends for snow removal. Georgie gave me one of the tickets, instructing me to be at the hiring hall in Coney Island at seven o'clock that night if I wanted to be hired the next morning. I wrapped my legs with burlap bags and arrived at the scene thirteen hours early—only to find myself fifth in line. By eight o'clock there must have been a thousand men hoping to be hired.

The temperature was bitter cold—eight or ten degrees below zero—and like most of the other men, I was inadequately dressed to spend the night outdoors. I held my hands under my arms for warmth, huddling against the building with the other men, sharing our body heat in the hope of surviving. Georgie brought a paraffin-coated cardboard container of hot coffee which he shared with me, but that was all that went into my stomach that night.

Morning and the hiring boss arrived. "Only the first fifty will be

91

hired today," he announced.

As the word passed back, some of the men appeared almost relieved that they would not have to stay and work in the ice and snow all day, but others were very dejected because they had starving families at home, and the anticipated pay of fifty cents an hour was much more than the usual dollar a day being paid laborers.

My tedious and miserable job was chopping ice and making a path from the curb to the trolley stop. When noonhour arrived, I sheltered in a recessed doorway, and the proprietor of a nearby delicatessen asked me if I wasn't going to eat.

"I've been watching you work hard all morning," he said. "You need something on your stomach. Come with me and I will give you a sandwich."

My frozen spirits warmed a little, and I responded eagerly, "I sure appreciate that, and I will pay you as soon as I get paid."

I worked until five o'clock, walked home, had supper and went right back back to wait the night in line again for the next day's work. I stuck to this schedule for three days and nights, but on the fourth evening I hurt so badly from cold and fatigue that I didn't return other than to get my money the following day and pay the shop-keeper. I gave the rest of my money to Minnie for board; she gave me three dollars back for shoes, warning me not to tell Tony.

I wanted to work, but there were no jobs. When a friend of mine enlisted in the army, I tried to get in, too. But, at sixteen, I was too young. Then, deep into the depression in 1934, I tried to get into the Civilian Conservation Corps. Still too young. For some inexplicable reason I got it into my head to ask the principal at my elementary school to write a note saying I was eighteen. She was horrified, of course, and yelled, "How dare you ask me to perjure myself?" I had never heard the word "perjure" before, but I could see by the look on her face that I had better leave fast.

"I am just trying to find a job," I apologized as I backed out the door and ran down the hall, the indignant woman in hot pursuit.

The night of Franklin D. Roosevelt's first inauguration, Monti and I visited the local pool hall, a large upstairs room containing twenty-six tables. The table we were using was way in the back of the room, and I didn't realize, at first, that an armed man was holding the other players against the wall at the far end of the hall. "If you little bastards don't get up here in a hurry, I'm coming after you," a second man shouted, directing us with the barrel of his revolver.

Monti and I obeyed immediately, raising our hands above our

head, and joined the end of the line. I took my position next to Walter, an elderly black man that I knew to be a kindly gentleman. This was his night out and he always dressed in a suit and tie and carried a flashlight because he had to walk through an unlighted garbage dump to get back home.

A third armed man stood at the top of the stairs to prevent anyone from escaping, and it took a little while before we realized they were not robbers but police detectives looking for hoodlums who had committed a robbery in the neighborhood. One detective frisked everybody, and when he got to Walter, he found his flashlight. Flashlights, along with screwdrivers, pliers, and jackknives, were all considered to be burglary tools, so the detective accused the old man of being involved in the burglary.

Poor old Walter was frightened and shaking, and though the pool hall proprietor soon convinced the detective of Walter's innocence, the plain clothesman confiscated his light anyway, and moved on to me. "How old are you," he demanded, and I answered that I was twenty-one. "Twenty-one!" he scoffed, "You're not twenty-one!" Grabbing me by the shoulder, he pulled me out of the line, booted me in the ass and told me to get the hell out and never come back. Though it was cold out, I didn't even think to retrieve my jacket, and as I ran past the policeman guarding the stairs, he hit me with his open hand on the back of my neck throwing me off balance, so that I stumbled and rolled the rest of the way down.

Life looked more bleak and hopeless every day. Not only was there no work, now there was no place to hang out, either. The city had closed down the Blue Diamond Social Club, placing a large red sign on the door which read: "Closed by the Board of Health—Do not enter these premises." Our despair was lightened a little, however, when Mayor Fiorello LaGuardia got a crime prevention quota from the CCCs to clean New York City streets of incorrigibles. On a sunny spring day in April, the bright thought occurred to me to go to Canarsie to ask Father Appo, whom I had not seen since I was six, if he could help us get into the Cs.

Moishe, Charlie and I arrived after lunch, and Father was busy with a lot of mothers and their daughters as they practiced for their confirmation. It was obvious that we caught him at a bad time, but he sent us into the kitchen to be fed because we admitted to having had no lunch. Later, he gave us a note introducing us to the desk sergeant at the police station and requesting that we be put into the CCC program.

"Don't you kids have a job?" the sergeant asked.

"No," we all answered in unison.

"How would you like to go into the three Cs?"

"Great," I answered for all three of us.

I could scarcely contain my excitement as we proceeded to fill out the forms. I decided to tell them I was twenty-one because I wouldn't need anyone to sign the papers then. No matter that I was just sixteen and looked it.

The officer who helped me fill out the application didn't question me when I told him I was twenty-one, and I was *in*. Shocked and jubilant that there had been no questions asked, I could scarcely believe that I had a steady job, at last. The depression that had caused me so much grief and suffering now offered a program that was to send me in a new direction. This direction would, one day, take me to the White House Rose Garden.

6

A New Life in the Northwest

A Train Ride to the Pacific Northwest and a Ferry Ride to Whidbey Island

"Wait'll you get the hook! Wait'll you get the hook!" chanted the oldtimers who had been inducted twenty-four hours earlier as we newcomers marched to the dispensary. Although we were incorrigibles from the streets of Brooklyn who thought we were tough, many of us succumbed to the scare tactics of the kids who had already received their shots. Dozens of young men raised in an environment of crime and fear passed out on the steps of the dispensary at the thought of getting a shot.

Nobody knew where we were going until we got to the train two days later. Scrawled on the side of our Pullman car were the words "Anacortes, Washington." Since few of us were great in geography, we assumed a word had been misspelled and that we were going to Anaconda, an airfield outside of Washington, D.C. To our amazement, however, the train headed due west across Pennsylvania.

I was quietly happy anticipating this new adventure that was taking me from the slurs against Italians I had come to hate so much in the city. I had become reluctant to admit my heritage because Italians were all considered gangsters and ditch diggers. Even though I knew that many Italians excelled in art, science and athletics, I was still very self-conscious about my background. My parents were not only Italian—they were hillbilly Italians from the south. In New York it was commonly held that the illiterate Italians, Irish, and blacks were good for nothing except common labor, but even though my education was limited I had dreams of advancing myself.

There were about seventy-five of us headed west, and I volunteered to do KP. An army mess-sergeant was in charge of cooking which was done on two legless wood-burning stoves set in a bed of sand. My job was to peel potatoes and help serve, carrying large kettles of vegetables and salmon up and down the aisles.

95

As we were rattling through Montana on the third day of our journey, a well-dressed man boarded the train and told us we were going to a small town in the northwest corner of the state of Washington, the most northwestern state in the United States. This meant little or nothing to most of us because our experience had been limited primarily to New York and its environs.

The next morning, when the train stopped at Spokane, we were surprised not to see a single Indian or cowboy. Starting our climb into the heavily timbered mountains beyond Leavenworth, I anticipated seeing burly lumberjacks like those in geography books. Though no loggers were visible, I was elated at the sight of the forest giants on the west side of the Cascades. Imagine settling and working in this sylvan, untouched environment!

Traveling across the country that summer the weather had been hot and clear, but when we stepped off the train that first morning in Anacortes, a heavy overcast with slight drizzle greeted us. In spite of the weather, my spirits were high; I had the feeling that this was going to be the best thing that ever happened to me.

The small town of Anacortes was located on Fidalgo Island, the only one of the San Juan archipelago connected to the mainland by bridge. Here we were loaded into open trucks and driven along a hilly, winding road past small family farms hacked out of dense woods along the edge of beautiful Lake Campbell, which had a small island in its center. This lake, I was to learn later, was popularized by Believe It Or Not Ripley as a rarity because it contained an island on an island. At Dewey Beach, we boarded the five-car ferry, which was so far removed from the huge ferries plying the New York harbor we feared it might not support our trucks.

As the ferry pulled away from the dock, I was filled with wonder at the sign on a small squat orange building built on the bedrock outcropping of what I came to know as Blout's Point. The sign read: Blout's Bazaar—Candy, Oil and Other Stuff, and imagining there must be something exotic waiting for me, I decided to go back and explore the bazaar as soon as I got my first payday, never dreaming I would find a business that was no more exciting than the small country store it turned out to be.

I loved every minute of the ferry ride across the water from Fidalgo Island to Whidbey where our trucks debarked onto a small wooden dock leading to a gravel road winding through the woods. The closer we got to our camp, the more elated I became, knowing that in this place I would have decent work and food and shelter.

And, here, somehow I would be able to show people what I could do because in the deepest part of me I *knew* I had ability and skill if only I was permitted to use them.

Dropping down a narrow steep road we came into the campsite clearing. Even the dismal weather couldn't diminish the beautiful setting of Cornet Bay, our future home. I was assigned, along with about fifty others, to Roosevelt Hall where we were given mattress covers to fill with straw. There was nothing in the long room but double-deck bunks and two large woodburning stoves without doors. Next to my bunk was the *cubby hole,* a small open room where the two men charged with keeping discipline slept.

Though many of the kids were homesick, I wasn't. I had lived in so many homes and with so many people that I didn't have a close bond to anyone or any place. I accepted things for what they were, while at the same time, I didn't take shit from anyone. I was on the defensive, willing to fight for what I felt was right.

CCC toilet facilities were a surprise to us city kids because the revolting smell was something we had never experienced before. Housed in an open-ended shed, the toilet could accommodate about fifteen kids. On our way up to the *crapper* that first night, we decided we would surely not work the next day because of the rain. When it rained in New York, nobody worked outside.

I Chew Snoose and Blast in a Beautiful Place

The next morning, however, even as the rain continued, we were called out and issued a set of *tin* raingear because, as we were soon to learn, in the Pacific Northwest outdoor work goes on rain or not. Our new canvas clothing protected us from wetness, thorns and nettles as we walked through the woods to the job site. I was assigned to Isaac Love, the powder man.

"You going to be a man, you got to have some snoose," he said in his heavy Swedish accent as he proffered the small round can of Copenhagen. "Like this," he went on, showing me how to place a pinch between my gum and lower lip.

I was eager to do whatever it took to be like the local men who were known for being tough and strong, so I watched for him to spit because I needed to spit. He didn't spit, so I didn't either, but noticing him swallow, I followed suit. In about a half hour, I felt nauseated, began vomiting and soon started running from the other end. It was a month or two before I dared to take another chew.

Isaac taught me all about the powder trade, and when he left the job three weeks later, I became the "powder monkey." I was proud and a little cocky the day that the U. S. Department of the Interior cameraman came to photograph the largest charge that I ever set off. The drilled holes in the road we were building were charged with over a ton of dynamite, and I told the photographer to shelter with me behind a huge Douglas fir where he would have an unobstructed view of the blast. Before pushing the plunger that would set off the charge, I hollered "Fire in the hold" three times warning everyone around of the impending explosion. Letting go of the plunger, I hugged the tree feeling I was protected from the blast by its seven-foot bulk; the cameraman poked his eye and camera around the side. What I hadn't counted on was the debris that cascaded down upon us from above, showering us with small rocks and branches. This was long before the days of safety hats, but fortunately we escaped with bruises and minor scratches.

Before Isaac left, he not only taught me how to drill and blast and chew snoose, he also explained how powder men could get sick from the dynamite. In the process of peeling dynamite sticks and splitting them with a jackknife in preparation for tamping them in the hole, the nitroglycerin in the dynamite often gets on the powder man's skin, is absorbed into the body and results in a helluva headache. I thought that I might get an occasional headache, but it happened everyday. I often had to go to bed right after work without eating supper, but I never complained; I wanted to do a good job and was just glad to have the opportunity to work. Also, blasting gave me a feeling of importance because of the danger connected with it and because of the accomplishment I felt at actually building a road.

The road was the bridge head of two spans that would connect three islands, Fidalgo, Pass and Whidbey, and would put the little Dewey Ferry out of business. Our work site was high above the turbulent waters of Deception Pass. From the Whidbey side I could see snowcapped Mount Baker with its glistening glaciers and green foothills. A deserted prison camp clung to the sheer rock wall of Canoe Pass on Fidalgo Island, and I often thought of the prisoners who had worked there suspended halfway between the top of the cliff and the wild waters below. Imagining the conditions under which these men had lived and worked as they crushed rock for the early highways of Washington State made me even more thankful for my job and my freedom.

Almost every evening I hiked back to the work site to watch the eagles fish the waters far below. I marveled at the strength of those beautiful birds as they struggled with large codfish and salmon, following their flight until they landed in their nests built in the highest trees around. The adults looked very proud as the young ones feasted on the prey. I had divorced myself from Brooklyn so completely that now all I thought about was my work and enjoying every bit of scenery and wildlife that I could.

Even a New Accent and Vocabulary

At night I went to sleep to the sound of rolling waves, funnelled from West Beach through Deception Pass into our bay. On very still nights, I could hear the distant chugging of tugboats straining to move their log rafts across Rosario Strait. The sounds of the city disappeared completely from my mind, and I thought that I never wanted to hear sirens or traffic again. I was so taken by the beauty and silence of the Pacific Northwest that I wanted to really identify with the area. I started by deliberately losing my Brooklyn accent. I not only lost the accent, I also incorporated local idioms and the Indian words which were used in everyday speech there. We were called *cheechacos*, which is Salish for "newcomer," and I soon learned to say skookum chuck for "strong running water" and mowich for "deer," while a woman was a squaw or a klootch. "A couple a three weeks" or "a couple a three days" were measures of time, and directions were often given as "this a way" or "that a way." Logger's lingo included "hanging a guy" which meant to make a guywire fast from the top of a spar to a stump; "choking a log" or putting a wire strap around a log to be skidded out, and "the bull cook," who was the head cook.

When I became a high rigger, I also added to my Northwestern vocabulary. Our foreman, Earl Lamphear, took me under his wing and taught me everything he knew about tree climbing. Our assignment was to remove the "widow makers" or hung-up broken branches suspended over the newly constructed road. I had to learn how to splice cable, and this involved a "bull prick," used to separate the wire strands of a cable so they could be easily woven. Another addition to my vocabulary was "Molly Hogan," an eye splice that could be accomplished without a bull prick and is shaped like a woman's vulva.

When I questioned Earl about it, he explained, " Molly Hogan was *the* madame of all the whores on Seattle's Skid Road and was reputed to have had the biggest pussy in town."

At that point I looked down at the Molly Hogan I had just completed and, sure as hell, it resembled a huge snatch complete with frayed wires that looked like pubic hair. In addition to expanding my vocabulary, cable and rope splicing were to prove invaluable to me throughout the rest of my life as I worked in the Pacific Northwest logging industry and in Europe during World War II.

Mail Call

About half of our New York and New Jersey unit was made up of kids on probation or parole. When these young men entered the program, their case workers gave them assumed names—but their mail always came in their legal name. For instance, a guy we knew as John O'Brien might get a letter addressed to Stan Kowalski, and this would tip us off that he was a felon. The kids with these assumed names hated mail call not only because they were then discovered by their co-workers to be outlaws, but also because their caseworkers were always pressuring them by mail to get promotions, and there were almost no advancements to be had.

The non-felons among us always looked forward to mail call, however. My brothers never wrote, but I got letters regularly from Minnie, Tony's wife. One letter made me especially happy to be thousands of miles from Brooklyn. In addition to the five dollars that I had asked to be sent from my twenty-five-dollar monthly allotment that they were supposed to be saving for me, she sent startling news.

Dear Johnny,
Enclosed find the five dollars that you asked for from your account.
Everything is going well with us, and you are lucky that you are out there where you are. Your gang got into a fight with the Greeks again, and one was killed and one had an ear cut off and wound up in the hospital.
Your sister-in-law, Minnie

I wished she had written just *who* was killed and *who* lost the ear. And, though I was happy to get the five dollars, I was a little remorseful because I knew my total savings would be less when I got out of the Cs. As it turned out, however, after two years of hard work, I never saw a penny of my allotment. I am almost certain Tony played the ponies and lost it all.

Our entertainment consisted of going to a movie or a dance in Oak Harbor, a town of less than four hundred inhabitants—mostly Dutch. When fifty or sixty CCC boys arrived for an evening, it appeared that we were inundating their town, and the local people resented our presence. Dances were held at the IOOF Hall, a large wooden building that never did seem to warm up enough. Only a few of the more congenial girls risked criticism from their parents and peers and danced with us.

The Oak Harbor American Legion organized a smoker, where our boys challenged the local boys in a boxing match. Everything went well until about halfway into the program when the local referee made a bad call. This incited the kids from camp, and a riot broke out. We were outnumbered ten to one as folding chairs sailed through the air and fists flew. Even the women present participated in the fight, knowing we would not hit them. I turned at one point just in time to see a cute blonde swing a chair at me from behind. I warded it off with my wrist and arm, and took the chair from her. This young woman eventually married the camp doctor.

Our camp commander, Harry Liebe, was an ex-football player from the University of Washington who weighed at least three hundred pounds. He climbed into the ring and started pulling people apart. I was a CCC policeman, and though I had no real authority, I felt a responsibility to help calm the crowd; I joined him in the ring.

"Calm down," he shouted in his loud authoritarian voice. Then he ordered all the Cs to leave the building and report to the truck.

"Don't come back! Don't come back!" the Oak Harborites shouted as we left.

"We *won't* come back! We *won't* come back!" we chanted in return.

And we didn't. After that we made Anacortes our recreational headquarters.

Snowed In On Mount Rainier

It was Labor Day weekend, and we were headed for a climb up Mount Rainier. We sang "Silent Night" and "Sweet Adeline" as we bounced along in the back of the army truck anticipating our new adventure. When we stopped in Tacoma, our education advisor told us we were picking up two experienced mountain climbers at the Tacoma Ski Club.

At the trail head each of us was delegated to carry a number ten can of food under our arms along the hazardous burro route as no provision had been made for backpacks. Hiking for hours in the rain, we crossed Emmons Glacier after dark and, at last, exhausted and arms almost paralyzed, arrived at a bunkhouse which had previously served a silver mine. Years earlier the lumber for this building, its large cast iron stove and beds, had been carried up the precarious trail on the back of pack mules. The mattresses inside our two-story rustic building had long since disappeared, and before our weekend on the mountain was over, we were to discover where they had vanished so mysteriously.

After a midnight supper of pork and beans, we were sent upstairs to bed, and it wasn't long before the flatulence began. The beans combined with the low atmospheric pressure of the high altitude turned us into gas chambers as we began to fart and laugh uncontrollably. We just had to lay there and suffer it out because the single window did not open.

During the night it snowed lightly, and we awoke to a white camp. Going downstairs, we found no one was up, and we tried to open the door of the bedroom where our education advisor, his assistant, and the two mountain climbers had barricaded themselves. They were pissed off that we demanded our breakfast, so we went about making a fire ourselves, puzzling why they had locked themselves in their room.

At last the four older men stumbled sleepy-eyed out of their bedroom and fixed breakfast. After a hearty meal of hot mush and stewed fruit, we inadvisedly prepared for the ascent of the majestic mountain newly covered with snow. It was difficult to see very far ahead in the lightly falling snow, but we were able to follow the trail. When we arrived at the 10,000 foot level, the snow was falling heavily, and the decision was made to abort the attempt for the top.

Arriving wet, cold and tired back at the miner's lodge, we went to bed right after supper leaving the four men to themselves. Before sleep came, we smelled smoke. Exhausted, we hoped it would go away, but, at last, we knew something had to be done. Ripping the boards off the boxed-in chimney, we discovered sparks from a crack in the bricks had set fire to a an old mattress that had been disassembled and stuffed piece by piece into the wall space around the chimney—the work of pack rats.

The next morning we wakened to a terrific blizzard, the snow outside our lodge now hip-deep. We hit the trail as quick as we could, and though the snowfall lessened as we descended, the wind increased. Boarding the truck, we felt we were safe, but we didn't get more than a mile or two until we began finding trees across the road. And so it was all the way back to Tacoma. We would drive a few miles and have to get out to buck fallen trees so we could pass. Back in Tacoma, we dropped off the two mountain climbers who turned out to be not so experienced, after all, and headed home.

A couple of months passed, and this same educational advisor arranged a weekend beach party to include the Tacoma ski-club. Tents were set up on North Beach and a lot of whiskey was on hand. The assistant educational advisor decided the men were gay. He informed the camp commander, and the camp commander called in the sheriff, and the sheriff called in the FBI.

The party was well underway when the law arrived that Saturday night. We never again saw or heard of our educational advisor. Fortunately, such blatant sexual discrimination would not be tolerated today.

Average Weight Gain—Twenty-five Pounds

The hopelessness and poverty of Brooklyn where I had been shunted from one family to another now seemed far behind me, and I quickly made up my mind never to return. I loved the forests, the water and clean air of the Pacific Northwest. The unharried, unhurried lifestyle of the locals suited me just fine. They cooperated in cutting and hauling wood or putting up a building, and they shared their garden and orchard abundance. Locals weren't bothered if they didn't have a car to drive ten or fifteen miles—they simply walked.

The three Cs didn't give us much money to spend, so we fit in fine with the local lifestyle. The Corps provided us with all necessities—good healthcare, housing, and clothing. The pants originally issued to us were World War I surplus—"ankle chokers" so tight that we couldn't pull them on over our shoes. As soon as we could save enough of our five dollars per month spending money, we bought cream colored corduroys, instead.

But best of all, we had ample, if not always palatable food. Our mess sergeant was an Oak Harborite and former logging-camp cook, and he was allowed sixty-six cents per day per person to feed us. Once, when a good buy on eggs came along, he purchased more than could be used before they spoiled. CCC boys did the actual cooking, and due to their inexperience, one Sunday morning they served up soft-boiled rotten eggs. One by one the eggs were cracked open, exploding their pent-up sulfurous stink into the mess hall.

I had been looking forward to a good breakfast and this unpleasant surprise prompted me to offer an egg to my bunk mate, Moko, halfway across the room.

"Hey, Moko, try this. It's a good one." I threw the egg toward him before he had a chance to refuse. Moko clasped his hands to catch the fragile-shelled missile, and it crushed, the foul odorous liquid splattering over his hands and face as well as onto the table.

Returning the compliment, Moko fired an egg back. It missed me and hit Di Nunzio, triggering a full-blown food fight that we kids thought was hilarious. Rotten eggs and canteloupe flew through the mess hall and rained down from the open trusses of the ceiling. We had eggshells and juice in our hair, on our faces, and running down our chests by the time we ran out of ammunition and headed for the shower room to clean up.

But we were stopped by the bugler blowing assembly. Surprised, we lined up in formation before a very red-faced, angry captain.

"There'll be no more of this," he shouted. "If it happens again, I'll send you home!" He dressed us down in no uncertain terms, but promised to bring in an army cook from Fort Lewis to oversee the kitchen.

"And now, you get back to the mess hall and clean it up until I am satisfied that it is done right," he ordered.

When the new Lithuanian sergeant took over, the food was not only ample but gourmet: a different kind of soup for every day of the week—and always home-made freshly toasted croutons. There was roast meat every noon hour except Friday, when we had fresh salmon, halibut, or oysters. In those days, it was possible to buy a hundred-pound sack of oysters freshly harvested from Padilla Bay for a dollar, so the whole camp could be fed for five bucks.

No wonder, then, that I and nearly everyone else gained twenty-five pounds during our first month in camp.

Recreation Run to Anacortes

Anacortes was a fishing and lumbering town, and the people there were more used to transients than Oak Harborites. Salmon fishing was seasonal, with men coming from all over the west coast to fish Puget Sound and Alaska, so Anacortes residents were used to *cheechakos*. In summer, the town was a mecca for salmon processing on Puget Sound with such canneries as Farwest Fisheries, Sebastian-Stewart, Western Fisheries and Anacortes Canning Company.

There were also many lumber mills: Morrison Mill, Fidalgo Lumber and Box, Anacortes Lumber and Box and E. K. Wood Lumber, as well as nine shingle mills. Shingle weavers and sawyers were tramp workers, moving from one mill to another whenever the grass looked greener upriver or down south. Sometimes, there was dissension between the weaver and sawyer because the sawyer wasn't cutting a good grade of shingle. Then, the weaver who had the job of *weaving* the shingles into bundles, would walk off the job because he would make less money. So, shingle weavers and sawyers came and went around the Pacific Northwest. They were easy to recognize because none of them had ten fingers. Working close to the saws, they inevitably lost fingers or parts of their hands to the dangerous rotating blade.

Feeling comfortable in Anacortes where we CCers were more readily accepted, I went to Saturday night dances at the IOOF hall and movies at the Empire Theater. As the recreation-run truck driver and CCC policeman, I got in free. Whenever there was a dance, the city required that a special cop be hired by Shorty Cavanaugh, who ran the dance hall to earn a little extra money. The first person I met in Anacortes was Lawrence Pollard, the special cop hired to keep the peace. Often he would turn unruly CCC kids over to me to make sure I got them back to camp and kept them out of trouble.

On the Fourth of July, 1935, I met Doris and Phyllis Anderson at a dance at the Eagles Hall. The two sisters were dressed alike in white sailor dresses that, I was to learn later, they had made themselves. As Put Anderson's band struck up the first notes of "Paper Doll," I asked Doris for a dance.

"May I have the pleasure of this dance, Miss?" I asked as I had been instructed to do by the Camp Commander in our Wednesday night Social Ethics class. Then placing a white handkerchief in the palm of my right hand—as I had also been taught to do in order not to soil my partner's dress with perspiration,—I steered her on to the floor.

"Are you a CCC boy?" she asked.

"Yes," I replied. "I'm Johnny Bananas from Brooklyn." She looked surprised, and I supposed *Bananas* must have sounded funny to her. At least, it was a name she would remember.

Afterward, I returned her to her chair against the wall, and thanking her, I bowed politely—again following the commander's instructions—and complimented her on being a good dancer.

Really impressed by her dancing, I went once more in the subdued light of the rotating mirrored ball toward the attractive girl sitting alone in her white dress.

"May I have the pleasure of this dance, Miss?" I asked again.

As we waltzed around the floor, she asked, "Are you a CCC boy?"

I was surprised, but I again answered, "Yes, I'm from Brooklyn." I didn't add my name, thinking she would, at least, have remembered Bananas.

Many dances later, I realized I had been dancing with both Doris *and* Phyllis, and that the sisters delighted in puzzling me as to who was who. Though they were very much alike, I was more attracted to Doris, the older one, who was more outgoing and lively. Her rich brown hair was pulled back from her forehead and ended in soft curls about her face. She was slender, about five foot five, with beautiful long legs that caught my attention. But it was her eyes—her deep blue eyes—that set me to dreaming.

She was what I considered the right height for my five-foot-eight inch frame. I wondered what she thought about my straight brown

Doris Anderson, 1942

hair slicked straight back in the style of the day. And my eyes. They were pale blue compared to hers. I wondered what it would be like to hold her and kiss her.

Three or four of us CCC kids stayed until the end of the dance, missing the last truck that returned by ferry to Whidbey Island. There was just one way to get back to camp that night. We walked nine miles to the bridge under construction that would soon make it possible to drive from Fidalgo to Whidbey Island. The steel had recently been riveted together to form an arch one hundred eighty-five feet above the violently swirling waters of Deception Pass. A temporary two by twelve catwalk had been placed on the steel beams for workers' access. We decided that if they could walk it, we could walk it—never mind that it was dark and we were unaccustomed to such heights.

Maybe we started across this narrow walkway partly to show our bravado, but if we could cross safely, it would also mean we could have a couple of extra hours in Anacortes. Relying on our cat-eyes, we placed one foot firmly ahead of the other in the darkness high above the treacherous waters, no one uttering a word. Taken one step at a time, the walk seemed endless. When at last we reached safety on the Whidbey side, we gloated over our winning gamble knowing the kids back in camp would be greatly impressed by it.

On one occasion, however, we stayed in Anacortes overnight in luxury at the old Vendome Hotel on sixth and Commercial. Earlier that Saturday, Lou and I "broke the dice game" and decided to celebrate by going to town for a steak dinner and spending the night. We informed the rest of the guys that we were staying at the Vendome, and three of them decided to pitch in five cents apiece to help pay the twenty-five cents that the room would cost for one person. I would check in at the front desk to make my reservation, and when I had gotten settled that night, the others would sneak up the back stairs.

Lou and I walked the nine miles into town in the afternoon arriving at the Marine Club with our winnings of three dollars apiece and very big appetites. We ordered the thirty-five-cent steak special that included french fries, toast and coffee, and when we polished that off, we ordered a second steak special. The waitress could scarcely believe her ears, and when we both requested a third dinner, she almost refused to order it because she couldn't believe we were serious, or maybe she thought we couldn't pay for it. Anyway, we not only ate three dinners that night we pitched in our change and

107

bought a bottle of sloe gin to boot.

Since we were under age, we hid the bottle beneath a bush in Causland Park, and when our friends arrived on the recreation truck, we acted the part of big spenders and took some of them up for a drink. Feeling our oats, we went on to the dance hall, and all evening I anticipated a good night's sleep in a real hotel bed. When I finally arrived at my room, I found the door open and a couple of kids already sleeping in the bed. At one o'clock in the morning the suspicious owner appeared at the door to find a room meant for one occupied by nine half-drunk kids, and she ordered all of us to leave. After arguing that I had paid for the room, she acquiesced that I could stay—but the rest had to go. As soon as she settled down at her desk, of course, the boys drifted back, one by one.

In the morning we all shared one towel and a bowlful of water, and disappeared quickly through the rear exit.

A Jack-of-All-Trades

Besides being the powder-monkey, I was a truck driver and also something of an electrician, mechanic, carpenter, blacksmith and plumber. One of my jobs in the last department was helping to build a "modern" latrine: ten seats back to back above a rectangular tank that held about one thousand gallons. The system had a large cantilevered elevated dump bucket at one end that automatically emptied into the trough, flushing all the effluent out the drain pipe.

When the system failed, I was asked to find the trouble and remedy it. This meant hauling hundreds of buckets of crap down to the bay. A grapefruit, stuck in the outlet, proved to be the source of our trouble, and after several hours of work, the toilets were operating normally and everybody was happy again.

Two days later, to my surprise, I was called out of the morning formation and asked to join the officers standing in front of the group. I assumed that I was going to be reprimanded, although I couldn't think why. Suddenly the company commander, holding a large roll of toilet paper, began reading a commendation that had been signed by everyone in the company.

"We knew this was a nasty job, and you did it diligently without objecting or complaining. We all want to thank you for relieving us of our problems."

As I received the scroll, I wondered to myself if it was truly an honor to be recognized on a roll of toilet paper. But then the whole company applauded: I realized that for the first time in my life I was being complimented and appreciated for something I had done.

Courting in Anacortes

I was dating Doris Anderson quite regularly now. We always took in the Saturday night dances, family affairs with mothers, fathers, and kids in attendance. Women got in free, but men had to pay twenty-five cents.

The Anderson family didn't have a car, so I devised a way to disconnect the speedometer of the recreation truck I drove when I got to town, and went and picked up all five of them. Doris, Phyllis, and their mother rode up front with me, while father and brother rode under the canvas canopy in the back. They were glad for the ride because it was better than walking in the rain, and I was making points with the whole family.

Being a truck driver also allowed me to help the Andersons when I was called to haul kitchen supplies from Anacortes to a camp on Orcas Island. A troop train had arrived with a whole contingent of replacements, and the mess sergeant helped me load all of the surplus food on the truck. He also had a lot of split wood that he was going to throw out of the kitchen car, and when I told him I knew a family in Anacortes that could use it, he gave it to me.

When Mr. Anderson and I finished unloading the wood, I looked at the food. It was surplus, after all, just like the wood. "Can you use some eggs?" I asked.

"Sure," he replied, eagerly accepting the crate I pushed toward him.

"How about some butter and ham?"

"Great!"

"What about meat?" I went on, eyeing a quarter of beef that had been sent with me.

"Of course!"

"Well, go get a butcher knife."

When he returned, I cut the round, the sirloin, rump, and T-bones leaving a miserable string of leg and backbones lying on the truck bed.

The look of satisfaction on his face and his profuse thanks let me know that I was appreciated. Excusing myself because I had a ferry to catch, I left with him still thanking me.

Late that night, we arrived at Olga on Orcas Island, and the remaining supplies were unloaded at Camp Moran. Appearing at the kitchen early the next morning, I heard the cooks discussing the whereabouts of the food that was to have been sent over from the train. I was horrified to realize I had given away food that was meant for one hundred eighty-five kids, though there was no way that the food in my truck would have fed that many hungry people. I could not understand why there were not sufficient supplies in camp, since they knew well beforehand that a large group was coming in.

They asked, "Did you bring all of the food over?"

I lied, "Yeah. What's in the truck is what they gave me?"

Next Friday, when I went to pick up Doris, the family told how they had canned the meat and baked hotcakes with the flour and eggs. I sheepishly had to confess that the food had not been surplus and was intended to be used for supper and breakfast on Orcas. I was never too sorry about what had happened with that food, though, because in my courtship of Doris, I seemed to be courting a whole family—a family like I had never had before.

The Cs Are a Family, Too

The Civilian Conservation Corps came into being by act of Congress in 1933. The original complement was for five hundred thousand kids between the ages of eighteen and twenty-five, and the age was later lowered to seventeen. The original intent was to employ welfare kids, but it was expanded to include street kids like me. Each CCC member received five dollars per month for spending money and twenty-five dollars was sent home. This money was deducted from the welfare payment of the particular family, or was supposedly saved for the young man when he got out of the Corps.

And the food—for those of us who had been surviving on maybe a single bowl of soup a day—the food was unbelievable. Up to one hundred eighty-five kids a meal were fed right off the griddle or grill or out of the oven of a huge wood burning cook stove, so everything was fresh. Food wasn't stacked in a pan as in most military operations today, and there was all you could eat. Some of the kids put away twenty hotcakes and a dozen eggs with no problem.

And as in most families, fights were common among us, a most memorable one occurring one evening in the mess hall. Benny and Lou had an argument in the mess line that didn't quite result in a fist fight, Lou escaping Benny's attack by running up into the mess hall. He stopped just inside the door at the bread case where he picked up a large French knife and waited for Benny to come through the door. Luckily, Benny stopped outside and little Di, all four foot ten of him, came through the door instead. Lou made a roundhouse swing with the knife, barely missing the top of Di's head, imbedding the knife in the door casing. Di turned paper white, but Lou thought it was a big joke that he had scared the shit out of little Di. Benny, still today, thanks God that he delayed entering the dining room that evening because he would have been decapitated.

Though I worked hard and was happy with my lot, I also got in a lot of fights myself. One Saturday night at the dance with Doris, two of our boys came to get me to stop a fight because Angelo was going to beat up on little Di. Out on the corner of 6th and N, I found big Angelo threatening Di.

"Knock it off, you guys," I said, "You'll get arrested, and anyway Di's too little for you, Angelo."

"If I want to hit Di, I'll hit him, and if I want to hit you, I'll hit you," Angelo bragged.

I could not let this go by unchallenged, so I took Angelo on and knocked him out leaving him bleeding on the sidewalk, his lip and chin split open. The other guys took care of him as I went back to the dance.

"What happened?" Doris asked.

"I knocked out one of the guys who deserved it," I said.

"But your hair isn't even ruffled up." Doris was admiring.

"On top of that, he's the camp boxing champ," I bragged, happy to make time with my girl.

The next morning at breakfast Angelo appeared with his chin and lip bandaged. I apologized to him, and he apologized in return as we shook hands. "I had it coming," he said. Several months later when Angelo went back to New York, he still carried the scar.

We fought forest fires as well as each other. Called down to Freeland on the South end of Whidbey, we found a raging fire covering three or four acres of second growth and brush. Although I was truck driver, I was also asked to carry a back pump and patrol the fire break putting out sparks that jumped the trail. Through the dense smoke I saw a glow, and going in to quench what I believed to be the start of a fire, I discovered Charlie Burelli, a fellow CCCer, passed out on the ground. His smouldering denims were the glow that attracted my attention.

I called for help, and we dragged him out into fresh air where he soon began recovering. The ensuing vomiting made him more uncomfortable than the slight burn on his stomach.

At the end of the day, the fire was contained, and a grateful local farmer invited us to help ourselves to all the strawberries we could eat from his nearby field. We had not yet had any fresh berries that season, so we gorged ourselves on the delicious red fruit before heading back. Supper had been held for us at camp, and when we finished eating our main meal, the cooks announced dessert. Much to our chagrin, there was the biggest dishpan of beautiful fresh strawberries we had ever seen. Any other time, we would have relished them, and the cooks could not understand our lack of enthusiasm.

The CCC projects completed between 1934 and 1936 are still enjoyed by thousands of local people and tourists each year. We built sturdy log houses for the park superintendents at Bowman's Bay and Cranberry Lake, and public restrooms in those locations as well as at Rosario State Park. There were also attractive public kitchens with

Deception Pass, 1935

112

fine wood burning stoves and huge fireplaces around which families still gather for hotdog or marshmallow roasts or for comfort on a cool misty day. We also constructed the beautiful stone and log guard rails enjoyed by millions today along Highway 20 in the Deception Pass areas of both Whidbey and Fidalgo Islands.

Convincing greenhorn kids that the Corps would not accept anything less than perfection took a lot of work, but the excellent condition of these buildings and fences over fifty years later attests to their quality. Most of our work was overseen by skilled local people including foreign-born stone masons. We also handcrafted the hardware and hinges for the doors, and these remain in good condition even to this day.

In addition to the practical crafts that we CCC kids learned during the day, we had the opportunity to study at night with the camp education director. He was a licensed teacher who taught us mathematics, English or typing—whatever we wanted. Since many of us had no education beyond the eighth grade, some kids needed to learn how to write a letter.

Our camp doctor taught first-aid one night a week, and when he finished with us, we felt we could perform surgery if necessary. Add to this the social education we were getting from our camp commander ("May I have the pleasure of this dance, Miss?"), and the Corps was supplying us with much of what we needed to take our places as useful citizens in the outside world.

Each month our sergeant would strap on his forty-five revolver and go to the bank for payroll money. We were paid our five dollars in silver, and enough money for a hundred kids was quite a bag full.

With our spending money, we bought soap, toothpaste and cigarets. Most of us smoked roll-your-owns and could get enough makings to last for a month for under one dollar. Once in a while there was enough money for a five-cent candy bar, and we were always eager to buy civilian clothing. My friend Benny Colacino from Bayonne, New Jersey, helped me out. Somehow, Benny's family back home was in pretty good shape, so he got back his twenty-five dollars each month. His problem was that he would usually have it gambled away before he got it, and would have to sell his much desired brushed wool sweaters, suede jackets and cream-colored corduroys to pay his gambling debts. I picked up many items of clothing for as little as two-bits.

Not everyone took to the three Cs the way I did. Many kids went back to the city. But the program was a life-saver for me. It took me away from the potential bomb of Brooklyn, where I lived on a street that had two houses of prostitution, one counterfeit operation, three bootlegging establishments, and one gambling house—my brother's—within a block.

Here, everything was new to me, even the rainy overcast weather that is so typical of the Pacific Northwest. The climate was gentle, the winters never bitterly cold or the summers insufferably hot as they had been in the East. But the positive changes went far beyond the weather: the CCC was another kind of family for me. I was housed in comfortable wood barracks, fed ample good food, and educated. This program, which grew out of the depression that nearly devastated me, saved me from a possible life of crime and abject poverty.

7

Marriage, War and Confiscation of My Deer Rifles

I Get Out of the Cs

When federal appropriations for the program dried up, I stayed on—as did most of the kids—because, though we would get no money unless funds were renewed, we would get food, lodging, and a pullman ticket for travel back home. And if the government *did* renew the appropriations, we would get back pay. Funds were finally made available, but some months later I decided to get out anyway.

I knew I wanted to make the Pacific Northwest my permanent home, and, since I had fallen in love with Doris, it was time to get a job on the outside and settle down.

A Job and a Wedding

I was eighteen and had nine dollars in my pocket when I was honorably discharged from the Cs in late spring of 1936. Early morning I would go to Morrison Mill at the foot of fifteenth street in Anacortes and hang around the office with the other men looking for work. When everyone else packed up and left about eight-thirty a.m., I stayed on. After all, though the weather might be a little soggy, it was nothing like the weather I had endured in Brooklyn waiting in line overnight for a job.

I was down to my last fifteen cents the morning I ordered coffee in Curly's Cafe.

"Aren't you gonna have any breakfast?" Curly asked.

"No, I'm not hungry."

"What's the matter? You out of money?"

115

"Yup!" I admitted, somewhat reluctantly.

"I'll stake you to your breakfast," Curly offered. "Staking" was a common practice in those days to tide over miners and loggers who were down on their luck. When I told him I would pay him back as soon as I could, I had no idea that my perseverance at the mill was about to pay off.

All the other guys looking for work had gone home, but I was still hanging around about ten o'clock in the morning when Dewey McFaddan, the yard boss, came out.

"I've got some work for you for the rest of the day," he said.

In those days nobody asked what the work was or what the pay would be, so I just followed him eagerly as he took me over and introduced me to Walter Wagner, foreman of the chip storage bin. Walt told me to scoop the chips away from the conveyor and throw them as high as I could against the side of the building. When the conveyor shut down at noon, I didn't leave the site because I didn't have any money for lunch anyway. Later in the afternoon the boss came and told me to slow down; I didn't have to work that hard. I didn't slow down, however, because I was working at my pace. Perhaps that's why I was put on again the following Monday.

At the end of two weeks I was made boom man. My training in the Cs came in handy, because I was able to sort the different species of logs. In those days boom work was very hazardous. Every year six or eight boom men drowned in the Pacific Northwest. One day, I almost became one of them. I was spreading logs with a pike pole when the pole broke, and I fell headfirst into the water between the logs—which then closed together and trapped me by my ankles. Suspended upside down in this black water polluted with sulfite pulp liquor, I had no choice but to swallow it as I tried to free myself from the vise of the logs. All I could think of was what a murky death this was going to be—but then, with my last bit of energy I finally spread the logs.

About the time my head burst up from the water, my co-workers arrived shoving their pike poles toward me, helping me out of the polluted bay where small bullheads and Petrale floated belly up. There was no concern for pollution then, so all mill waste including pulp liquors, sawdust and bark were dumped into the water, fouling the bay and killing marine life.

In spite of the danger of the work, I felt fortunate to get a job at Morrison Mill. It was the steadiest mill in town, and, as it turned out, outlasted all the others. I also established credit at Allen's Mercantile,

116

as was the custom. Everyone charged whatever they needed and paid their bills on payday. When my future felt secure and I had saved the great sum of twenty-four dollars, Doris and I decided to get married even though her parents weren't too crazy about me. In spite of the fact that I had tried to become part of the family, they were Scottish and Protestant while I was Italian and, they figured, Catholic.

They agreed, however, to go to Mount Vernon with us for the wedding, Doris's father driving us around town in his green Dodge to find a place for the ceremony. We came upon the Baptist minister mowing the lawn in front of his church, and he said he would marry us within the hour.

As the minister disappeared into the parsonage next door to the church, I mentally recalculated my funds. We had spent twelve dollars for the first month's rent of our apartment which included all the wood we could burn, and Doris had held out for a seven dollar ring. The license had cost us two dollars, and I was planning to give the preacher the accustomed two dollars for the ceremony. That would leave us with one dollar until next week's payday. When the minister reappeared, however, freshly bathed, shaved and dressed in a fine suit, I was so impressed and grateful that I decided to pay him three dollars, and then we were broke.

The wedding was as unpretentious as our pocketbook. No flowers, no special clothes, Doris wearing her best dress and me in my cream-colored corduroys. Nervous and anxious to get the ceremony over with, I said "I do" before I was supposed to, sending Doris' younger brother and sister into an outburst of giggles.

Back at my new in-laws' home there seemed to be no preparation for a celebration. Perhaps their lack of enthusiasm about having me for a son-in-law, coupled with their poverty, made a party out of the question. Doris and I decided to walk over to our new apartment where I cooked a wedding supper of spaghetti and meatballs. The wood cookstove snapped and popped as we discussed plans for our future.

"As soon as we get enough money, I will buy a fresh ham and make Italian *prosciutto*," I said.

"And I know how to can, so we can put up tomatoes, corn, peas and beans," my new wife said. "There'll be lots of peaches, pears and plums, too."

We were feeling very comfortable beside our own warm fire in our own place. Tony may have gambled away my CCC money, but

117

I knew we could take care of ourselves.

Like a couple of squirrels preparing for a long winter, we continued to make plans as we waited for the charivari promised by some of my co-workers. When the noisy crowd did not materialize, we went off to bed in our sparse surroundings. What happiness not to have to get Doris home by midnight!

The very next day we began scrounging jars that could be used for canning. Crescent coffee jars were especially desirable for peaches and pears; their wide mouth and square shape allowed the fruit to be arranged in an eye-appealing display. We also used the jars for preserving the old canner cow that I bought for seven dollars. This meat was so tough that canning was the only way to tenderize it. Doris and I labored all day, and when the last jar of meat was finished, we tossed the remaining bones and yellow fat into the large copper boiler. We added every kind of vegetable and seasoning, making a gigantic delicious-smelling minestrone, envisioning soup all winter long. Then, exhausted, we decided to wait till the next day to can it.

Too late! When we awoke in the morning, our noses told us that our great kettle of soup had spoiled in the night. Doris and I were both near tears as we watched our winter's sustenance flush down the toilet.

A Beauty Shop and a New Home

Doris completed her apprenticeship as a beautician and borrowed eight hundred dollars from People's Bank to set herself up in business, her uncle Fred Fisher co-signing the note. The Kulshan Beauty Shop only brought in enough money to make the loan payments, pay the rent, buy supplies and keep her in clothes. But there were side benefits. Mrs. Massey, who had a ranch on March Point, traded fruit and vegetables for beauty work, and a Dutch lady whose family had a turkey ranch on Whidbey Island bartered a turkey for a permanent every Thanksgiving. I drew the line though, when one evening Doris came home with two bartered squabs, still in down, for me to butcher for supper.

About this time we also bought our first house, just two doors away from the house where Doris had been born. At four hundred dollars—five dollars down and five dollars plus interest per month—this was a real bargain. It was complete with hot and cold running water, inside toilet and bath, and the seller threw in a wood burning cookstove. We were in heaven! And heaven was really brought close to us at night, when lying in bed we could see clear through the wide cracks of the dry shiplap ceiling and the missing shingles to the starry sky.

During that first winter, we nailed a blanket between the kitchen and bedroom because there was no door to close, and the only heat we had was the cookstove. It was bitterly cold outside, and before going to bed I set a kindling fire, so I could jump out of bed in the morning and quickly light it and return to bed until the kitchen warmed up. I also let the water run in the sink so the plumbing wouldn't freeze up. In the morning I friskily jumped out of bed, dashed into the kitchen and went sliding on my ass across the floor. The drain trap had frozen under the sink, causing the trickling water to spill onto the floor and freeze into a miniature ice rink.

When spring came, I put in a garden. I planted pole beans in circles, placing willow saplings in the center for the plants to climb up. Several mornings later on my way to the woodshed, I noticed the beans I had planted sticking up above the ground. Thinking that the rain had washed the soil off them, I stopped to poke them back in. This continued for four or five mornings, and one day Doris called out to me, "What's taking you so long to bring in the wood?"

"The goddam beans won't stay in the ground, and I'm pushing them back in."

"They're not supposed to stay under ground. That's the way they grow, you nut."

A week later, I realized that I had killed most of the bean seedlings, but the willow poles were sprouting into a dense forest.

Depression Desperation

I had always lived with hunger and poverty, managing somehow to keep myself alive, but now marriage brought obligations for Doris as well. Strikes and jurisdictional disputes made it difficult for me to get a full week's work at the mill, so when Doris's uncle gave me a magazine advertising how to get rich raising mushrooms at home, I fell for it. Borrowing ten dollars from Uncle Fred, I sent away for the kit and converted the garage into a mushroom cave. Weeks passed with no sign of a mushroom. After several months, I realized that I had been bilked by a scam and wrote to the man in Seattle who had sold me the worthless brick of hardened clay that was supposed to contain mushroom spore.

I called him every name I could think of, said if I ever got to Seattle I would work him over so he would never forget it, and even went on to threaten his life. Several months later when I received a letter from the postal inspector, I feared I was going to be prosecuted for threatening a man's life. I learned, however, that many others had fallen into the mushroom trap. The postal service had indicted the con artist and were asking for any evidence that I might have that he had used the mails to defraud.

Those days were the very depth of the depression, and when Harold Springer asked me if I thought we could get a deer at Deception Pass Park, I assured him we could. We decided to talk to Judge Al Sallenthin at city hall before going on the illegal hunt. We arrived at the judge's chambers above the fire department to find the Chief of Police, Harold Hinshaw, with the justice.

"Judge, things are getting tough. It's hard to get a full week's work because of the strike situation, and we cannot get welfare, so we are going out to the park to get a deer." I laid it on the line. "You can either arrest us now or wait until later, but we are going out to the park and shoot a deer."

The judge and chief looked at each other in surprise, not uttering a word as Springer and I turned and left.

Because I didn't own a gun, Springer let me use one of his.

"Hesitantly handing a rifle over to me, he asked, "Are you sure you can shoot this?"

"I've shot a .22 lots of times."

"Now this ain't a .22. Be careful, and make sure you only shoot at the deer."

Within two hours we had our deer. Small as it was, it was still a deer although some people called Whidbey Island deer overgrown jackrabbits. We never heard from the law, and, when the deer was all consumed, we were relieved because the evidence was gone.

While Harold and I were out hunting, we had discussed the need to put our energies into far-sighted activities instead of such stop-gap measures as illegal deer and oysters.

Harold said: "The union leaders at the mill want us to change affiliation from the AFofL (American Federation of Labor) to the CIO (Congress of Industrial Organizations)."

"I'm willing," I said. "Maybe it will stop all of the jurisdictional disputes, and we can get a full week's work."

Under the AFofL, the different crafts would decide on their own to go on strike and expect support from everyone else in the mill. The workers all honored the picket line, so our work was very unsteady. We felt that if we could all join the CIO and be represented by one union, problems could be resolved easier—one contract would cover everybody.

A dozen or so of us took the job of organizing the timber workers into the CIO—among them Paul Kreuger, Bill McNutt, Wes Collins, Harold Springer, Merton Perkins, Vern Sumey and myself. Many men at the forefront of this movement were avowed Communists, but not in the sense of overthrowing the government. These men had joined a party that promised more for workers. They wanted steadier work with some kind of job security and better pay. For example, some of the local fishermen knew that one of the mill bosses liked wine, so they kept him in Dago Red to insure a job for themselves when they returned from fishing in Alaska in the fall. The conscienceless boss would fire good workers and hire his pet fishermen leaving many men without work all winter. The saying was, "If you don't part your hair right, you'll get fired when the fishermen come back."

It took several months before we got a majority to swing over to the CIO. This majority vote caused the AFofL to bring goon squads up from Seattle and throw jurisdictional picket lines around the mill. When we heard that district AFofL president Joe Skovich had decided to visit Anacortes, we knew there would be another picket line next morning. The whole town was suffering from these strikes. When mill workers did not get paid, the merchants who staked them did not get paid either. Harold Springer and I decided to take matters into our own hands.

As soon as it got around town that Skovich had parked his Dodge sedan in front of the New Wilson Hotel and checked in with his wife, Springer and I went to have a little visit with Mayor J. George, who was also fed up with all the loss of work.

"We're gonna give Skovich until nine o'clock tonight to get out of town, or we will run him out," I said, noting that it was about five-thirty then.

"Yeah," Springer agreed. "We're gonna run him out of town, and we would like the police to be busy elsewhere when we do."

"No problem, boys," the Mayor said as he picked up the phone and gave the operator the number of the police station. "Chief, I want you to see to it that none of our police are available for the next few hours. A few CIO boys are here, and they plan to encourage Skovich to leave town around nine o'clock tonight—before he can strike the mill tomorrow." When the mayor put down the phone, he turned to us saying, "Funny thing! It seems no one knows where any of our police are, and there's no chance they can be found until well after nine tonight."

With the support of the law, we went back to the hotel and had a talk with Skovich in the doorway of his hotel room, his wife peeking around from behind with a yapping pet poodle in her arms.

I said: "We're sick and tired of jurisdictional lines, Skovich. We want you to leave town by nine o'clock tonight, or we will drag you out behind a car."

He bristled: "Listen here—I'm a citizen and have every right to be in this town for as long as I want."

"And we are citizens that have the right to work without your interference," Springer snapped` back at him.

Skovich went into his room, slamming the door behind him. We retired to the lobby to wait. By then a crowd was gathering outside in the street, blocking traffic and forcing cars to detour around the block. When seven o'clock rolled around, and there was no sign that Skovich was making a move to leave, we wanted to go up to his room again, but the hotel management would not allow it.

"He's been making phone calls," the desk clerk said. "He couldn't get hold of any of our local police and when he tried to get the sheriff to come over, the sheriff said he couldn't because he hasn't been called by us. Skovich is on the line now to the state patrol, but they won't come because they haven't been called by the Anacortes police for any assistance, either."

When the line was clear, I phoned Skovich and reminded him that it was after seven o'clock, and he had better start packing. Still he was adamant that he would not be run out of town by any number of toughs. The crowd outside continued to grow, and by eight o'clock there was a lot of fist shaking and hollering. Springer and I began to worry that the unruly crowd would get out of hand.

Another call to Skovich warned him that we were having trouble with the crowd, and he had better get out while the getting was good. By a quarter of nine, just when we were really beginning to be apprehensive about the crowd, Skovich and his wife came down the stairs; we held back the townspeople as he got into his car and drove off. As far as I know, he never again visited Anacortes.

There was still trouble up the Skagit River. The Lyman local, mostly loggers, had voted for CIO affiliation because this union was against the men being paid according to the number of board feet of timber they fell and bucked. This was called "busheling," and it was a slave type of operation where a man could kill himself trying to make a living. For instance, loggers would spend half a day to fall a tree that turned out to be "punky" or "conky," and therefore was graded so low that they wouldn't get paid for it.

The main aim of the CIO was to replace this kind of piece work with negotiated hourly wages and better working conditions. The AFofL threw jurisdictional picket lines around the operation, however, and, as in Anacortes, the workers respected the picket lines. Nobody wanted to be a "scab." Logging operators became fed up with the illegal lines and locked out everybody, including the district president, Karly Larson, an avowed radical. Karly called us in Anacortes and invited us to help with the dispute.

Two carloads of us arrived at the dingy Lyman union hall where Karly greeted us with his usual cud of snoose tucked in his lower lip. The rest of the boys, huddled around the wood burning heater, were arguing the merits of the CIO versus the AFofL because a few diehards had not yet switched to the new union. Karly called the meeting to order and talked for thirty minutes without spitting snoose once, trying to convince the AfofL holdouts to swing over.

Then we took turns trying to convince them to all pull together and eliminate most of their troubles. As the evening wore on, tempers began to flare and some of the more unreasonable men announced that they were going to go to work and start falling trees, lockout or not, picket line or not. We pointed out to them that they would probably not be paid even if they did work, and they could even be arrested for trespassing. Finally, we calmed them down and convinced them to settle their differences by all joining the CIO.

Even after I began getting a full-week's work, we were still in the hole because everything was on credit, and—like everybody else—Doris and I had overextended ourselves. Tony Campano's stepsons, the three Allen boys, and I often launched a rowboat at the Swinomish Slough bridge and went out to raid the unclaimed oyster beds in Padilla Bay. Roy Mesersmith, his brother-in-law, Don Toogood and I cut wood on Widow Douglas Almond's land at Alexander Beach on shares. The beautiful widow took a shine to the handsome Don. One day when she came to inspect our wood cutting operation, she pretended to slip. Falling to her knees in front of Don and reaching up in her most coquettish and appealing manner, she asked him to help her. We always told Don he missed the chance of a lifetime by not carrying through with the wealthy widow, but he was virtuous and true to the young lady he was going to marry.

I also tried to earn money through another woodcutting venture. Frank Giesler, who owned an eighty-acre ranch near Lake Campbell, heard that Roy Mesersmith and I were willing workers. He offered us some huge old-growth windfall fir, seven and eight feet in diameter, if we would help him build a road into the woods with his team of horses. This wood was so fantastic that it is unthinkable in this day and age that we used it for cooking and heating. These firs had blown over as much as a century before and had settled a foot deep into the soil. The wood was preserved in excellent condition, however, because a fire prior to their falling had burned the bark off, seering the sap and encasing them in a protective shell. We could never earn more than eighty-five cents a day bucking and splitting those logs, but, in addition, we got our own wood.

We had a little box trailer that I towed behind my Chevy coupe to deliver the wood, and when I drove by John Weir's place on Heart-Lake Road, he noticed I did not have a license for the trailer. He was also selling wood and reported me to the local cop, Marvin Beebe. Marvin lay in wait for me and told me that I would have to get a license or stop hauling wood.

"Marv, I don't have the money for a license—I'm barely eating— and I'm not about to stop hauling wood. If you arrest me, I'll lay it out in jail. I don't have the money to pay any fine," I said angrily.

Marv continued telling me I could not drive that vehicle without a license, and I told him I was tired of listening to the bullshit.

"Take me in and lock me up now because I'm not going to quit." I said. Marv walked off mumbling, but fate was on his side because shortly after the car died from the beating it took up in the woods.

Catching and selling crab was another sideline. Since my car had pooped out, I often hiked the two and a half miles out of town to the Burlington Northern trestle that ran across Fidalgo Bay, carrying two large crab hoops on my back. Baiting my traps with free meat scraps from Guy Hurd's butcher shop in Allan's Mercantile, I set them out, built a driftwood fire under a boiler full of sea water and sat down to wait.

The wait was never boring because it was so beautiful sitting on the tracks surrounded by the peaceful bay, snowcapped Mount Baker in the distance and March Point right in front of me. This gentle farming peninsula, shown on early maps as Marsh Point, later became March's Point after Fred March, an early day settler. It was then completely pastoral, with a few stump ranches where the mill

124

workers lived and supplemented their income with milk cows, chickens, pigs and a garden. It wouldn't take long, watching the panorama and daydreaming, before my traps would be so full that I could barely lift them onto the trestle. When I got about fifty legal crab, I cooked them, put them in a burlap sack and toted them into to town. I got five cents apiece for them in the beer taverns until somebody informed the game warden that I was selling crab without a license.

I also beach-seined illegally with Frank Voyvodich in a twenty-foot open skiff powered by a Star engine that had been cut in half to make it a two-cylinder power unit. We managed to put this boat on a reef twice, and one time we were so loaded with dog fish that the tide carried us out into the strait. When the tide turned in our favor, we were able to get back to the fertilizer plant with our catch. Frank and I realized that we weren't making any money in spite of all the work, and if we continued, we could lose our lives. Before that happened, we decided to take the boat's life. We chopped a hole in the bottom, pushed it off the beach into Guemes Channel, and watched it slowly disappear beneath the waves.

The salmon run had really hit, and I was looking for work at Western Fisheries with Bill and Chet when the boss, Bill Parks, came out and offered us a job pitching fish. This work was usually done by Indians in those days; it was considered too menial and dirty for Caucasians. The pay was good, however, and we accepted gratefully even though we were expected to work round the clock until all the fish were unloaded. Bill and I pitched the salmon out of the hold onto the deck of the Kasaan where Chet relayed the fish onto the conveyor belt that carried them up into the cannery. About one o'clock in the morning we realized we were up to our knees in fish *gurry* (fish slime, blood and seawater) and Bill yelled in alarm, "Hell, this boat is sinking!"

"Chet," I called up anxiously, "look over the side and see if this boat is sinking."

"It sure as hell is," he called down to us. "The goddam water is up to the gunnels."

The elderly engineer was called out of bed, and one look down into the engine room told him that he had forgotten to close the sea cock. As he scrambled down into the flooded compartment, we untied the Kasaan and began pulling her around the dock to the beach to prevent her from sinking in the deep water. When the boat settled on the sand, we expected the engineer to appear. When he didn't, we looked down the companion way to discover that a five-gallon can of gasoline had upset, asphyxiating him.

Leaving Bill and Chet to muscle the old boy out of the cluttered engine room, I ran to the office to call the fire department—only six blocks away—to come with the resuscitator. Fireman Shorty Strom responded immediately, driving the windshieldless truck full-speed downhill towards the dock as fireman Milton Cookston cranked the hand-operated siren. Seeing them speed through the empty streets, I knew they were going too fast to stop. Afraid for my life, I waved my arms wildly, jumping out of the way as the fire engine slammed on its brakes and skidded out of control across the wet wooden dock. The front wheels leaped the heavy timber bulkhead, and the truck came to a tenuous halt, teetering precariously above the icy waters of Guemes Channel. Scared shitless, the two firemen—still seated in the truck—started blaming each other for their predicament.

"Knock off the bullshit," I hollered. "Get the resuscitator and follow me. There's a man dying out on the boat."

Fortunately, the engineer had recovered by the time we arrived, and we took comfort in the fact that he was going to live.

Our grueling fish-pitching job lasted for forty-eight non-stop hours, and when we were finished, we received the unheard of amount of seventy-eight dollars. This allowed Doris and me to square up all of our bills, vowing never to go in hock again.

War and Anti-Italian Feeling

It was 1939, and the economy was looking up. Hitler had started his conquests of the countries bordering Germany, and there was great demand for Sitka spruce to build up the Luftwaffe. Since Italy was trying to expand out of Italian Somililand, she was buying our timber to build planes in her fight against Haile Selassie in Ethiopia. Britain, The Netherlands, France and Belgium also began expanding their air forces, which created an even bigger demand for this strong lightweight lumber.

I was still working at Morrison Mill when a shift was added just to cut airplane lumber. Some of these spruce logs were more than thirteen feet in diameter and so huge that they had to be drilled and blasted with black powder in order to pass through the throat (guides) of the head saw. The finest grades of this wood were sawed into flitches or rough-sawn timbers and shipped to Europe. The leftovers went into making refrigerator frames, piano sounding boards and box shooks (parts).

It was a welcome sight to see the Model-T Ford jitneys driving down Commercial Avenue towing ten or twelve wagon loads of box shooks in tandem like a trackless train. They were headed to the port dock at the end of this main street, where the shooks would be stacked in warehouses to await a tramp freighter. Most of these components were shipped to Shell and Texaco refineries in Mombasa, Africa; there they were assembled, filled with two five-gallon cans of lube oil and sold throughout the world. The demand for these timber products created steady employment in Anacortes and was a great lift for a town that was all but dead a few years earlier.

Our personal economic position improved greatly, too, and I managed to buy a Model-A Ford for twenty-five dollars. Owning a car allowed us to travel around the northwest part of the state with our friends Roy and Mabel Mesersmith, and to do some gold prospecting. We would pitch in our money for gas until the tank gauge showed half-full, so we would be sure to have enough left to get us back home. When we reached our destination, we would untie the sluice box from the fender, and unload the chicken we had butchered earlier along with the rest of the picnic supplies. Then Doris and Mabel built a fire and prepared the meal while Roy and I prospected the creek. At times, a good show of gold in the Cascade River would excite us and tempt us to do it for a living, but I always remembered what an old prospector had told me years earlier. While I was still in the Cs, I met an old man with a bushy white beard and crumpled felt hat leading his heavily laden burro down Burpee Hill out of Concrete. He could have just come out of Death Valley.

"Have you found any gold?" I asked.

"Yup, there's gold everywhere in these creeks and streams," he said, "but it's very fine and very scarce."

"I would like to do some prospecting myself," I went on.

Perhaps the old man recognized me for the greenhorn from the city that I was. He warned," Son, if you find anything don't take it seriously, because there's more money lost in the search for the yellow stuff than there is made. If you've got a job, stay with it."

So although we prospected every creek in the Skagit and Skykomish basins, we never allowed ourselves to fall prey to "gold fever."

As times continued to get better, I saved enough money to buy a nice little Jersey cow for twenty dollars. Roy agreed to take care of the cow on his fifteen lots, and we would share the butter, cream and

127

milk between the two families. I also bought weaner pigs which Roy and Mabel raised on the skim milk, so this gave us our meat as well as dairy products.

The cow's name was Daisy, and she was as gentle as her name. When after a few months her hormones began flowing and she started what we called *bulling,* Roy and I walked her a couple of miles up the road to the Duranceau Dairy to be bred. Lorene Duranceau had us turn Daisy loose in a small electric-fenced enclosure while he brought his prize bull, Pierre, to the farmyard boudoir. Closing the fence behind Pierre, Lorene held onto the bull's lead chain, holding it high above the electric fence. The three of us watched intently as the two animals became acquainted and Pierre mounted Daisy. Lorene became so excited he dropped the chain onto the electric fence.

"Goddam, that fence, " he screamed as the jolt hit him, throwing him to the ground.

Lorene's predicament was nothing compared to what happened to Daisy and Pierre. As the electricity hit them via the chain, both animals fell to their haunches, bellowing and snorting. Wild-eyed and frantic, each must have thought this the most ecstatic sexual encounter ever. Daisy scrambled to get out and away from under Pierre, and Pierre was just as happy to let her go.

It soon became obvious that the two animals had lost interest in the project, so we opened the gate expecting to put the chain on Daisy and lead her back home. The little cow had other ideas. Apparently blaming us for her painful and embarrassing experience, she bolted past us and headed for home on her own.

During her next heat, Roy and I again took her up to the Duranceau farm to see Pierre. But, unfortunately, both animals had been indelibly imprinted with the earlier encounter and would have nothing to do with each other, so we headed immediately down the hill to the Dixon Farm. Bob Dixon assured us his fine bull, Buck, could breed our cow and the fee would be "two dollars just like it would be in any sporting house." I winced at the sight of this big old Holstein bull, at least twice the size of our little family cow, but Buck was our only hope unless we wanted to take Daisy five miles out to Summit Park.

Buck and Daisy were put in this very small board enclosure that looked like a rodeo chute. Little Daisy appeared calm and expectant, and she looked lovingly at Buck with her large brown eyes. But this ancient decrepit bull didn't excite very easily in spite of his owner's claims, and Bob felt compelled to assist in the matter by rubbing Buck's protruding vertebrae with his cane.

"Maybe you'd better rub his balls," I suggested. "That's where his sex organs are. Not his backbone."

But apparently Bob knew what he was doing because, at this point, Buck decided to mount Daisy and consummated the act. We paid the two dollars and took Daisy back home, Bob's final words ringing in our ears: "I guarantee Buck's potency. If it doesn't take, bring her back—no charge."

Nine and a half months later, Daisy presented us with a little bull calf, Henry. When Henry was weaned, Roy said, "Before you take him to pasture at your place, we'll *nut* him."

Placing little Henry's head in the stanchion, Roy seated himself on a stool behind the calf while I held the tail out of the way. Roy opened his pocket knife and quickly slitting the bag squeezed hard, popping the nuts out of the incision; then he cut the cords.

I was quite devastated because Henry humped up his back and was looking back at us and bawling. However, I was from the city and had to take the advice of an expert in animal husbandry.

"That's it," Roy said.

"Aren't you going to sew his bag up?"

"No, it'll be OK. I've done thousands of 'em." Of course, he exaggerated.

"Well, the least you could do is put a couple of band aids on it."

"Hell, we'd be the laughing stock of the island if we did that. Henry'll be OK," Roy said with finality.

The next day Henry was feeling OK just as Roy had predicted, and I took him home. When the time came, Henry was butchered, shared between the two families and canned. He had been our little pet, and it was hard to eat him, but hunger took precedent over sentiment during the depression.

Nonetheless, things continued to improve. Realizing that the house we were living in was beyond repair, we used our steady and larger income to bid on two adjoining lots that had been Henry's home and were up for tax-title sale. I offered ten dollars for each lot, and Charlie Dean, the clerk in the treasurer's office, refused it, demanding a twenty-dollar minimum for each to cover the cost of advertising the sale. I grudgingly accepted and paid my forty-dollar deposit. Before the auction, I contacted Wallace Sharpe, the county commissioner, and asked if I would have any trouble winning the bid for that price because my funds were limited. He assured me that there would be no opposition, and to keep his promise, Wallace talked to Mike Demopoulis and Emil Schrieber, two local business-men who always bid on every piece of tax-title property. Conse-quently, there was no opposition to my bid which sailed through in less than a minute. Doris and I were elated to be the owners of three lots and began making plans to build a new home immediately.

The blueprints for a five-room house cost me fifteen dollars at Tucker Lumber, and twelve thousand feet of shiplap and structural lumber, a further two hundred dollars. I was happy to spend all my spare money and spare time building this house and watching it take shape—a dream come true. I had put over a year into it and was shingling the roof when Doris came out one black Sunday morning and called up to me that Pearl Harbor had been attacked by the Japanese.

"I don't believe it," I shouted down to her.

""Well, it's true," she said. "Come on down. President Roosevelt

North Cascades, 1940

130

is on the radio now."

I got into the house just in time to hear Roosevelt say something about "this dastardly attack by the Japanese." What would happen now? I was deferred from the draft because of my work in a critical industry, but this direct attack on the U.S. put things in a different light. I felt sure that sooner or later I would be drafted, but I was not ready for the incident that occurred the next day and decided the matter for me.

A couple of years earlier I had bought two rifles: one from Dr. Frost and one from my co-worker, Len Lobdell. The Frost rifle was a little lever-action Winchester carbine that had notches on one side of the stock for elk he had shot and dimples on the other side for deer. The other rifle was a 30.06 sport model Winchester and came with eight hundred rounds of World War I ammunition which I intended to use for deer hunting. The day after Pearl Harbor—Monday, December 8—Marvin Beebe, now assistant chief of police, appeared on the log boom where I was working.

"Come over here," he called gruffly, not addressing me by name even though he knew very well who I was. "I want to talk to you."

My mind was spinning as I bounded from one log to the other before I could face him on a solid float. "What's wrong?" I queried, deducing from his urgent manner that he had brought news of an accident to Doris or some other mishap. He looked at me very sternly without a smile and said, "We, the police department, have been told that you have two rifles and a lot of ammunition, and we want it."

For a minute I couldn't answer. What bastard could have turned me in for having legitimate hunting rifles and ammunition which I intended to use for sport? My mind was swimming as I tried to figure out what this was all about. Perhaps because of my union activity, I was being discriminated against, but, then, since I had heard so many slurs against the Italians, I decided the police were taking my rifles because of my heritage.

"And what if I don't give them to you?" I said angrily.

"We'll come and take them," he threatened with a smirk of revenge, knowing that this was one time that I couldn't challenge his authority.

I started thinking of Doris, knowing that if I refused, things could get worse. I had heard talk of moving Americans of German, Japanese and Italian backgrounds inland so they would not be near the sensitive coast.

"OK," I said reluctantly, "Come and get the goddam things at home after I get through work tonight."

I insisted that Beebe give me a receipt for my guns and ammunition that night, so I could reclaim them after the war.

There weren't many Italian families in town, but names like Luvera, Premo, Simaz, Dorbolo, and Campano come to mind. When I ran into Tony Campano a week or so later, I inquired about his three stepsons, the Allen boys with whom I had gathered oysters who were then stationed with the army in the Philippines. Tony, always happy to talk with me because I spoke Italian, told me that they hadn't heard from the boys. But he went on to say that the police had been to see him, too, warning him that he might have to move inland. Tony lived a very meagre existence, supporting himself and his family with a small truck garden. He asked no one for help, though he needed it because he had been wounded and crippled in World War I as a soldier in the American army. Shortly after local "patriots" had threatened Tony, a veteran's group came to his aid and backed them off. This group even saw to it that Tony finally got a disability pension, albeit more than twenty years late. Subsequently, his three stepsons lost their lives in the Philippines, so Italian-American Tony Campano paid his dues in full to his adopted country.

The anti-Italian attitude became so vehement that I decided to volunteer for the army engineers and show the self-proclaimed patriots that I was a loyal American who would do a good job defending our country. I boarded up the windows and doors of our unfinished house and bid goodbye to Doris and the Pacific Northwest. As I climbed aboard the stage to Fort Lewis, I wondered if I would ever again see the woman and the small town I had come to love so much.

8

With the Army In England

Shipped Overseas in Seven Weeks

At Fort Lewis, eight or ten of us were assigned to fill chuck-holes with gravel when the anti-Italian feeling surfaced again.

"Those goddam Dagos can't be trusted. They're nothing but gangsters and gandy dancers," one guy said.

"Yeah, we've got to get over there and clean 'em out," another said.

I listened for some time, getting madder and madder, until I finally declared that I was of Italian parentage, "—and I'm as good an American as you guys."

That ended the conversation. Ten minutes later, the guy who had been most vitriolic swung his pick and shattered a small rock, part of which flew up and smashed his eyeglasses into needle-like shards. Slivers of glass were embedded in his eyeball, and I warned him not to close his eyelid or touch his eye. After assisting him to the first-aid station, I never saw him again, but I was certain that this unfortunate incident finished his army career.

At noon hour we were surprised to see Sally Rand, famous from the Chicago World's Fair for her artistry with fans. She'd come to visit her husband Tuck Greenough, an inductee ready to be shipped out. They sat together eating in the mess hall, and we scarcely recognized her with her clothes on.

Though I only stayed two days at Fort Lewis, I soon saw how men avoided being transferred out to combat units. For instance, a sergeant would ask if any of the recruits had experience in tailoring or pressing. Those who volunteered would be put to work in his barrack tailor shop pressing and altering the poorly fitting class-A uniforms that were issued to us. These recruit helpers received no pay, of course: the money went to the entrepreneurial sergeant, who in turn probably paid off his superiors.

The second day, when about ten of us climbed aboard the covered army truck with our barrack bags and orders, we ran into another quick-buck operation. While the truck driver revved up the engine signaling us to hurry because the train was waiting at Nisqually, a GI from finance quickly handed us some money and asked us to sign a receipt for it. Before we had a chance to count this money—to be used for meals—the unscrupulous GI waved the driver on. We were sent off with just about a dollar a day for food. Since most of us would be traveling by train, where meals were expensive, this was grossly inadequate. I realized we had been ripped off because I knew the government was allowing a minimum of four dollars a day to eat. Probably this kind of racketeering happened at military posts all over the country.

At Camp Claiborne in Louisiana, I was assigned to the 342nd Engineers. We were placed in quarantine and began our basic training in a desolate, snake-infested swamp area. There weren't enough rifles to go around, so we were issued tent stakes to patrol our area. Les Wilder, also from the Pacific Northwest, and I pulled guard duty one night and about one in the morning Les began yelling.

"Corporal of the Guards! Corporal of the Guards! Help! Post number one."

Fortunately for us, armed only with wooden stakes, the infiltrators were not spies, but emaciated wild pigs trying to make their way to the garbage cans down by the mess hall.

Finally we were issued our personal gear and rifles, and began typical infantry training. This included twenty-five-mile hikes, one of which ended in a torrential rain. Arriving back at camp exhausted, hungry and wet, we found not a single tent standing. The guy ropes had shrunk in the steaming downpour, pulling all the stakes out of the wet sand.

Things got worse. Day after day we were sent on "problems" carrying a full field pack, including all four blankets, knowing we were not going to sleep out —and would be unable to use them even if we did because it was so hot. We were also ordered to carry our cumbersome gas masks although we knew there would be no gas attack.

One particular morning, however, the order of the day did not require us to bring our gas masks. Our problem that day was to assault a hill, behind which was the second battalion of our regiment. Advancing in a skirmish line, we formed just below the crest and were ordered to attack. As soon as we went over the hill, we were surprised by the would-be enemy who stopped us dead in our tracks with smoke grenades and shells. With no gas masks for protection, we made a hasty retreat, gasping for fresh air and struggling to see out of tear-blinded eyes.

As soon as we were able to clear our throats and eyes, we began demanding, "Who the hell fucked up on this one?"

"If we're gonna fight Germans, we'll never win the goddam war this way," I said.

"This is typical of the army," another voice complained. "Situation normal, all fucked up." The voice belonged to a Private Cramoga, and the look of agreement that passed between us was the beginning of a long and close-working partnership.

Our new officers had all been recruited at Coulee Dam and turned out to be construction people given commissions without any military training. These men didn't know how to wear their hats or even make up a pack, and they looked pretty ridiculous. The cadre that came with us from Louisiana was made up primarily of Pennsylvania National Guardsmen, and they helped the new officers shape up. These cadremen had just been elevated as leaders and given stripes, and they took advantage of their first authority making it as miserable for us new recruits as possible. A number of us became very angry with these would-be leaders, boasting that when we were aboard ship, we would throw them over the side if they ever came above deck.

When our quarantine was over, we moved on to Fort Dix, New Jersey. Our work here consisted of post security and practice boarding ship on a simulated gangplank, so we assumed the time was getting short, and if we wanted to visit nearby family or New York, we had better get on with it. Because we were all restricted to camp, the Charge of Quarters gave us all the blanks we needed, and we wrote our own passes.

Deciding to pay brother Tony and Minnie a visit, I wrote myself a pass to Brooklyn where Minnie was surprised and happy to see me.

"Your brother is at the Coney Island Legion Club—gambling," she said. "Come, get in my car, and we'll go find him."

Climbing to the second floor of the club, we stopped at the landing, and Minnie beckoned to Tony playing poker in the far end of the room. When his hand was finished, he came over, impatient because we were interrupting the card game.

"What the hell are you doing here?" he inquired abruptly. "Didja eat?"

135

"No," I said.

"Take the kid out for something to eat," he ordered.

And that was all there was to the short and none-too-sweet farewell from my oldest brother as I headed off to war.

An English Ship and a Prat Boy

The Duchess of Bedford was to be our home for the next ten days. Alongside us in the slip was the French liner *Normandie,* which had burned during repairs and now lay helpless on her side. She was eventually raised, re-named the Lafayette, and became our largest troop ship.

The *Duchess* came to New York from Singapore, where she had taken a bomb on the stern. Repaired and converted to accommodate five thousand GIs instead of seven hundred luxury passengers, she was anything but luxury for us. The officers got the best quarters, sleeping on cots in the dry covered swimming pool, while we dogfaces were assigned rope hammocks and unimaginably cramped quarters. The cabins were stifling hot on that summer day. They already smelled so strongly of sweaty woolen uniforms and body odor that I knew sleeping was going to be almost impossible. The toilet, a wooden shed built on the fantail of the ship, accommodated about forty or fifty men at a time, a steady stream of water flushing the effluent that collected in the trough directly overboard.

I was happy to pull guard duty the first night aboard because it took me out of the foul smelling hold. There were no lights or whistles as the tugs silently eased us out of the slip into lower New York harbor, and it was my duty as Corporal of the Guard to clear the decks and enforce total blackout.

Making the rounds, I noticed a light coming out of the skipper's cabin door which was ajar, probably due to the heat.

"Turn off these lights and keep this door closed," I shouted gruffly as I stepped inside.

Totally unprepared for the apparition that appeared from the shadows, my jaw dropped as an emaciated old man in short black pants and white ruffled blouse came scurrying toward me, obviously quite alarmed.

"Shhh! You'll disturb me Master," he whispered in a strong Cockney accent, wagging his index finger back and forth in front of his pursed lips.

"Jesus Christ, what is this?" I was incredulous at seeing an elderly man in a boy's outfit. Then I realized that he was a prat boy: the last of a vanishing breed that had begun during the days of sailing ships when parents would actually sell a nine- or ten-year-old boy to a ship's captain. The lad would be paid a few dollars a month to perform all household and sexual duties for the master of the ship.

This prat boy still dressed as he did when he was a child, though he was in his sixties. He wore black patent leather pumps with large silver buckles and sagging white stockings that climbed his skinny calves and disappeared just below the knee under the cuffs of his velvet knickers. His blouse, scruffy and in obvious need of a wash, was in keeping with the pale gray skin of his wrinkled face.

As soon as I gained my composure, I repeated my order. This time, however, I spoke more quietly and added "please," so that it sounded more like a supplication than a command. I was that stunned at the sight of a prat boy grown old.

The dense fog lifted about noon on our first day out revealing the flagship *Texas* off our bow. She was towing a paravane, a floating tube that was used by the lead ship in a convoy to indicate speed or direction change. A British Marine was posted twenty-four hours a day on the bow of our ship to observe the paravane and keep in telephone contact with the pilot house. This method of communication was necessary because of total blackout and complete radio silence.

A column of destroyers on each side of us made us almost impenetrable to the wolfpack of German submarines patroling the North Atlantic. On our starboard flank, the battleship *Nebraska* mothered us like an old hen protecting her little chicks. It was very comforting to know that such a huge armada of both British and American naval ships were escorting us—the largest troop and cargo assembly to that date.

About five days out of New York, the cargo ships headed northeast toward Murmansk, Russia, as we continued southeasterly toward what we suspected would be England. Several months later, we learned the ships that left us had become the ill-fated July Fourth convoy that lost ninety percent of its vessels. Unchallenged, the German Luftwaffe—for which I undoubtedly helped provide Sitka spruce—chose their own time and place to pick the ships off like sitting ducks as they made their way through the North Sea.

Aboard our ship were the advanced cadres who would arrange for their parent units to come at a later date. Among these advance troops there were about fifty men of the Fourth Ranger Battalion, the most elite, rugged group that I have ever seen in the military. Of the five thousand men aboard, these volunteers were the only gung-ho men, the rest of us merely following orders and pretty unhappy to be going overseas.

Daily exercise helped to keep our spirits up, and on one of my walks around the deck, I encountered a familiar face.

I said: "Weren't you the commander at the CCC camp at Deception Pass?" "Yes, and now I can place you," he said. "You were there too, weren't you?

"I sure was. You probably remember me as Johnny Bananas."

We talked for about half an hour, catching up on what had happened to each of us. Robert Brown was now a Major and an aide to Colonel Kermit Roosevelt of the First Infantry Division.

"Johnny, do you want to come into my unit? If you do, I guarantee you a commission when we get where we're going," Major Brown said. "I'll make arrangements for the transfer, if you're interested."

I was pleased at the offer, but after thinking about it for a few minutes, I decided that I should stay with the group for which I had volunteered. Somehow, I felt fate had relegated me to the engineers, and I should not change.

As the ship sailed closer and closer to the war zone, Colonel Roosevelt assembled the troops on the deck for a pep talk. He was a small man, not at all like his husky father, Teddy. Kermit Roosevelt was known to be a hard drinking brawler—his squashed nose was the proof—and that day his appearance was even more remarkable. Because his own raincoat had been stolen, he wore a borrowed raincoat that reached down to his shoe tops. Standing close to the rail on the deck above, squinting through the rain, he shouted how important we were and how our wives, girlfriends and mothers were all proud of us and waiting for us to return.

"Now, you know we are in submarine-infested waters," he concluded," and that there's a good chance we will be sunk. If we are hit, I want you men to know that I will be the last one off this ship, but be goddam sure you go over the side in a hurry."

This bit of humor lightened our situation, but not much. No matter how many jokes were told or how much praise was handed out, we were well aware of our danger. When an unidentified airplane appeared on the horizon, about a day out of England, we were pretty apprehensive until we recognized it as a British Sunderland flying boat. Circling, it dipped its wings in friendly recognition.

An English Ship and a Prat Boy

The last day of our voyage took us down the north Irish Sea on our way to Liverpool. This waterway was cluttered with sunken ships, and it seemed to us our captain was using the drowned masts and superstructures as buoys to guide us into the harbor. The destruction was unbelievable. We had read and heard about the Battle of Britain, but our trek through this watery graveyard brought Britain's suffering home to us.

Apparently the British were not prepared for our arrival. We were told to stay aboard for another night, so those of us topside went below to our sleeping quarters. Early on in the trip, four of us had opted out of the airless tomb to which we had been assigned, hanging our hammocks on a steam line in a small companion way. Since we had pulled our guard duty that first night, we were not missed. Our sleeping conditions improved and so did our diet.

Tommy Burns, the youngest among us, was an experienced thief who, early on, managed to steal a whole roasted turkey from the officer's mess. Later he stole two boxes of apples, and we were seated on the floor munching the much-appreciated fresh fruit when the air raid sounded. Our first reaction was relief that we were in the companion way, surrounded by the steel hull, which would act as a bomb shelter should the ship be hit. Relief faded to horror, however, when the crew slammed the water-tight doors shut, sealing us off from the rest of the ship. We realized that we would die slow deaths of suffocation if our vessel joined the other sunken hulks at the bottom of the harbor. Fortunately no bombs fell nearby, and after an hour that seemed like an eternity, we heard the all-clear sound.

Our First Billets on Salisbury Plain

We were bound for Perham Downs, in the South-central area of England known as Salisbury Plain. Midway in our journey, the train stopped briefly at a station where English ladies boarded and served tea. No doubt about it, now; we were truly in England. These ladies obviously knew better than to ask anything about who we were or where we were going. However, a woman on the platform came up to the window and called in, "Are you Germans?"

"Hell, no!" Lou retorted, miffed. "We are Americans."

She backed away, apologizing and mumbling something about helmets. Apparently our pisspot-shaped steel hats looked a little like German military head gear.

We were met by British officers and an army band that marched

139

us in full gear to our billets. *Marched* is not quite the right word. Rather, because our step did not fit the fast British rhythm, we bumbled along at our relaxed pace.

The second morning it became obvious that the secret of our arrival had not been kept. The German Luftwaffe pulled a low-level strafing attack, hitting the barracks next to mine. Since the air raid warning didn't sound until after the raking was all over, it was sheer luck that no one was killed. This was the beginning of many aerial attacks that kept us up all night. Each time the air raid sounded, the machine guns had to be carried half a mile to the top of a knoll. These were water-cooled Browning .30 calibre weapons that required four men: one to carry the gun; one to carry the tripod; one to carry two cans of water; and another to carry the ammo. By the time we got these pieces set up and ready to fire, the Germans were headed home and the all clear had sounded.

We would no more than get back to the barracks and into our sacks, when this futile routine would have to be repeated. After several weeks of this charade, we returned to the barracks to discover Bob Tie, who had not participated in his assignment, was drunk and had shit himself in his bed. Our barracks were completely blacked-out, without ventilation, and the stench was so revolting that six or eight of us dragged him out, mattress and all, and left him under the stars. Though we were happy to be rid of him, he had the best of the deal. He was breathing fresh air while we had to use our lungs to filter the putrid smell inside.

Because our American rations were late arriving, the British were charged with feeding us. Since we knew the British didn't have much to eat, we were willing to accept thin oatmeal porridge without milk or sugar and a half-slice of bread deep-fried in animal fat for breakfast. Other meals usually consisted of Brussels sprouts, a small piece of potato, or peas that had been allowed to grow very large to increase the yield. Leaving the peas in the field for so long also allowed time for the pea weevil to lay eggs in the plant, and this resulted in a worm in every pea. The night of our food riot, we were served mutton stew with peas. It was too much for us. The stew had been allowed to go sour, and to make it worse, each pea had yielded one worm that floated leisurely on top of the stinking mess.

When one of the men at our table turned the serving pan upside down, men at other tables followed. We walked out, cursing the rotten food. An hour later, our battalion was marched to a gymnasium where machine guns had been set up at every corner. The

140

adjutant brought us to attention and the regimental commander read the riot act to us, finishing with the threat, "Yours was a mutinous act, and if you do it again, we'll use these machine guns on you. We officers eat the same food as you."

Pointing to one of his lieutenants, he ordered him to tell us what they had been served for supper.

"We had mutton stew and cake for dessert."

"Cake?" we dogfaces hollered back in unison. We had never been served a dessert. Obviously embarrassed, the colonel dismissed us, and only the two leaders of the riot were given time in the brig. After work, the rest of us would go and visit the two who were paying the penalty for something that we were all involved in. Strangely, they didn't seem to be in any hurry to get out. Then they explained: they had been assigned the terrible duty of cleaning the NAAFI building, which employed three young attractive British women. The two prisoners and their guard were having sexual liaisons with these girls every morning after the work was done.

Fortunately, it was not long until food began to arrive from the States, and we were able to enjoy American rations. We also were issued gas protective gear because the British felt sure that the Jerries would launch a gas attack. Equipment also came at this time, and I was assigned to a bulldozer which had no seat. In addition to fashioning a wooden seat for the machine, I bought tools with which to repair it from the local ironmonger and began studying the diesel engine repair manuals, so I could keep the beast running.

My first job was scooping out a trench for the steel columns of what was to be a large ordnance building. We fashioned a crane by attaching a telephone pole to the dozer blade and raised our trusses in record breaking time. Working from daylight to dark, we completed the steel work in two weeks; this was the first of many record-breaking accomplishments for our unit.

Exhausted from the hard work, only a handful of us signed up to go to a dance at the RAF airdrome at Andover. Our officers pressured us to go and show our appreciation, however, so finally about twenty-five GIs went. The British were always surprised to see U.S. commissioned officers and enlisted men at the same dance because these two classes never mixed at their functions. No matter that we were tired: there were about five WAAFs to each American! They didn't hesitate to tell us that "Americans are fascinating," wanting to know what part of the *colonies* we came from. My answer always was that after the Revolution there were no more *colonies*, only *states*.

This was our first introduction to the women who were to make us feel welcome and relieve our loneliness far from home.

The nearby village of Tidworth had been completely taken over and turned into a military cantonment. Row houses became barracks for the First Infantry Division, and the finest old home was turned into a Red Cross club. It was more than a coincidence, perhaps, that the Red Cross director turned out to be Mrs. Kermit Roosevelt.

Another famous name appeared at Tidworth. Fred Astair's sister, Lady Adele Ashley, soon joined Mrs. Roosevelt as a British volunteer with the Red Cross. Lady Ashley greeted the boys, and as her part in the war effort, offered to write letters home for them.

To The Cotswolds

The Cotswold Hills, in Southwestern England, were a great improvement over the barren chalk downs of Salisbury Plain. Here, slow streams were green with watercress, and winding footpaths offered a quiet invitation for walking and bicycling. This was fox-hunting country, and, occasionally a huntsman in colorful habit appeared in the landscape, his well-groomed mount surrounded by a pack of beagles on their way to the hunt. The dogs clustered tightly around the horse's hooves, and all moved together as if they were one unit swooping across the countryside.

It was also in this rolling green countryside that I came to understand the groundsheets that some British women carried rolled up behind their bicycle seats. It made little difference whether it was daylight or dark, lonely GIs and lonely English women held their trysts on these waterproof covers under the Cotswold sky. Perhaps sex is freer during wartime because we deeply sense how tenuous life is, or perhaps it is nature pushing and shoving to replace the lives that are being lost to this mad activity of the human race. Whatever the reason, I pass no judgment in this matter. We made love out of our hearts; we made love out of our desperation.

Seeing the location of our new project from a distance, we thought it was just another charming Cotswold hill. Instead, it turned out to be a masterful structure built by the British to conceal the Allied Forces trans-Atlantic radio transmitter and antennae. Made of chicken-wire and dyed burlap, it was very difficult to discern from the natural topography. Now we Americans took over and installed diesel electric generators to power the secret project.

There were civilian radio technicians from the U.S., GI MPs, and a dozen of us engineers. We ate our sandwich lunch in a small tent, and although we worked together and could see what each was involved in, we were forbidden to discuss any phase of the operation; we talked about other things. We Italo-Americans learned that others in the group, members of the Masonic Lodge, were conspiring to defame and vilify us.

One night on our way back to Cheltenham, where we were headquartered, we decided to work over one of these Masonic cadremen, and we beat him up pretty badly. Subsequently, our company commander transferred all of the cadremen except the first sergeant out of our unit, and we never saw them again.

Not only had prejudice against Italians followed me overseas, but news of someone out of my childhood as well. Al Lianza was sitting on the cot next to mine reading his mail, when he sadly exclaimed, "Holy Christ! Father Appo died."

"Did you say Father Appo? The priest?" I wondered if I had heard right. "I knew Father Appo when I was a little kid, before I went West." Our Italian heritage had brought Al and me together; our old priest's death deepened our friendship.

Al and I remembered Father Appo as an outstanding man—tall, handsome and dark-skinned. We shared the common belief that he was of American Indian parentage. Whatever his background, we agreed he stood head and shoulders above the other priests, not only in physical height, but in refinement. His lavish lifestyle was in contrast to his humility, his loyalty to the church—nevertheless, like most of his parishioners, we admired him greatly.

Years later, for the purposes of this book, I made some inquiries about Father Appo's background. I was very surprised when a Catholic archivist described him as "famous, notorious, and unique." I discovered he had been educated in Rome—which explained his flawless Italian—and he was not of Native American heritage. Father's family was originally from Haiti. Birth and death records indicate the family crossed over the color line in the late eighteen hundreds. Father Locksley Appo may well have been the first black priest in the Catholic church. And though there is mystery about the man's heritage, there is no mystery about his refinement and goodness.

It was December, now—our first Christmas away from home. Instead of Christmas cards, many of the men were beginning to get "Dear John" letters, which were always discussed after supper in the barracks. At a public dance at the Cheltenham opera house, I met Eric, an English sailor, and his wife, Doris, who invited me to their home for dinner. Eric and I attended a rugby match before the meal—my first and last game of rugger. It looked to me as if somebody blew a whistle and they all rushed at one another and ended up in a big heap.

Two days after Christmas we were ordered back to Perham Downs. We knew from the stockpile of arms and ammunition and the huge influx of Americans that the invasion of the continent was imminent—and that we were going to be part of it. The night before leaving we sat around, depressed, discussing what we were going to do if we ever made it back home.

"What will you do, Al?" I said, thinking that he would say he was going to consummate his marriage. He had sneaked away from Fort Dix for the ceremony and returned immediately, never spending any time alone with his new wife.

"I'm going to go into the electrical contracting business," he said.

"Well, aren't you gonna take time to go to bed with your wife before you go into business?" I was trying to help us forget our predicament.

"Ah, shit, there's plenty of time for that, Big Nose," he said, grabbing the end of my nose and twisting it between his thumb and index finger.

"Hey, Clyde," I called across to the Okie, "what about your wife? How come you got drafted when you got a nine-year-old daughter?"

"I got divorced," he said.

"Why'd you get divorced?"

"Well, she had the claps."

"Did she give you a dose?" By now everyone was listening intently and forgetting the war for a moment.

"No," he said.

"Well, how did you know she was clapped up?"

"Well, I know because I seed her pussy, and I know'd she had the claps." Ending the matter, he went on to another subject. "I always have trouble with women. Even here in pubs when I go to piss after a couple of beers, the woman I've been with is gone, and I can't figure out what's wrong with me."

Clyde was a little pinched-faced fellow about five-foot-five, illiterate, and anything but a ladies' man. I suggested that he just "sweat it out instead of pissing it out."

Now it was my turn to re-direct the conversation. "What did you do for a living back in Oklahoma, Clyde?"

"I was a dishwasher in our little diner, but when I get back from the war I want to be a dishwasher in a big hotel in Tulsa," he said.

Al asked me if I was going to go back to the Northwest or bring my wife to Brooklyn, and I assured him I was going to go back and finish the house the war interrupted and settle down.

"I don't intend to die working on a log boom. I'm going to go into another field that has more of a future," I said. Remembering my childhood, I continued, "I want to help people if I can. There'll be a way."

"Put the lights out," Passman hollered to DeForest who was near the light switch.

"Shoot the goddam things out," DeForest shouted back, too lazy to get out of his bunk.

At the suggestion Billy Fender, an ex-professional boxer who had taken too many blows to the head, loaded his M-1 and fired a couple of rounds through the roof. For fear that Billy might shoot one of us next, I went over and calmed him, taking away his rifle.

Perhaps it was due to the chaos of leaving the next morning that Billy was never reprimanded.

A Secret Mission to Wales

Lou, Al and I decided to visit Southampton to see for ourselves the devastation that the Luftwaffe had wreaked upon the largest seaport in Britain. We were wandering through the most heavily damaged residential area, where nothing remained except a church and a bank, when we met an English gentleman, a block warden, who described what had happened when a parabomb, or blockbuster, made a direct hit on an air raid shelter.

"The shelter was filled with about five hundred people—mostly women and children who were trapped in the rubble," he said. "We tried to dig them out, but the rescue crews were overwhelmed."

"What happened?" we asked. "How did you get them out?"

"We couldn't get them out. There was no way we could get to them. The cries and moans of the injured and dying were so terrible and hopeless that we pumped ether into the rubble to relieve their suffering." This was our first experience of war as it kills innocent women and children.

When another American engineering unit was relieved of their

145

duty because the steel structure they were erecting went out of plumb, ten men from our unit were chosen to repair the listing frame. Lieutenant Stone, the officer to whom we were assigned, was a twenty-one-year-old shoe salesman only recently arrived from Florida.

"These men are experienced and know what they are doing," our company commander told the young lieutenant. "Just give them their heads."

At the site, Tony Caliendo, Walt Cramoga, and I surveyed the job and decided how we would proceed to straighten three hundred feet of roof trusses that were four feet out of plumb. Before climbing up into the structure, I cautioned the lieutenant and the rest not to do anything while the three of us were working above.

We straightened one truss, secured it, and moved on to the next before we noticed our new lieutenant had not followed orders. Going with some men to the far end, he cut one truss loose causing all of the trusses to collapse in a domino effect toward us.

As the other men hollered, we saw our predicament, and decided that rather than drop thirty-five feet to the ground, we would ride the twisting steel to the concrete below. Fortunately none of us were injured because the steel stopped about ten feet above the ground. Dropping quickly down, I started for Lieutenant Stone with Walt and Tony close behind me.

"You dumb son-of-a-bitch! I told you not to do anything! I'm gonna knock your goddam head off," I shouted, lunging toward him, my early lessons learned on the streets of Brooklyn coming to the fore.

Tony grabbed me, warning, "You'll go to jail if you hit him, Johnny."

"I don't give a shit if I do," I ranted, knowing that our lives had been put in jeopardy, to say nothing of the embarrassment we would have to face due to the failure of our job.

I calmed down, however, and we returned to the company headquarters to face the music. Surprisingly, we were not reprimanded, and we never went back to the job. Soon after this, Lieutenant Stone was reassigned to another unit, while Browning, the truck and trailer driver, and I were given a secret assignment.

Told nothing more than to pack all of our gear, load the bulldozer, and be ready to leave at five o'clock next morning, we suspected something big was in the wind. We knew that a beachhead had been established at Casablanca, so we thought we might be going to North Africa. The question was why we two were the only ones from Company B of the 342nd engineering regiment singled out to go.

British MPs riding motorcycles led us from our area to a main highway where the convoy of six Diamond-T trucks towing lowboys loaded with bulldozers was assembled. Meandering slowly through the sleepy villages, Browning and I discussed whether or not we were leaving England and wondered if we would ever join our parent unit again.

"We're obviously going into a combat zone, and our chances of making it home are getting more remote every day." I was becoming increasingly demoralized with every mile.

"I wonder if our wives will be waiting for us if this continues," Browning said, making me feel even worse. "This thing could go on for years at the rate it is going now."

Every six or seven miles the MP leading us was relieved by another rider. At first, we didn't understand what was happening. Finally, we realized that none of our leaders knew what our destination was either. They were merely responsible for escorting us for a small segment of the trip.

As dusk fell we were shunted into a muddy lane under trees that would camouflage us for the night and then isolated behind barbed wire from anyone who might talk to us. Our travels the next day were a repeat of the day before with complete secrecy not only about where we were going but about where we were. During the war in England all road signs had been removed, so we did not know until we arrived on a dock early in the afternoon that we were in Barry, South Wales.

Again we were put into an enclosure, this time beside a ship tied to the dock, and it became apparent that we were going for another boat ride. The next day we helped load our equipment on the ancient tramp steamer, feeling we would be fortunate if it floated long enough to make its destination.

As we waited orders to board ship, we witnessed the taunting of a Welsh soldier by half a dozen English troops.

"You're never going to be anything but a bloody coal digger," they mocked.

"Leave me alone," he begged, tears streaming down his face. He was small and obviously not too bright.

"Why don't you lay off him?" we shouted out from our barbed wire enclosure.

147

But, of course, they didn't pay any attention to us Yanks. And this incident was not the first time I'd seen weak people tormented in the military. In our own company, our frail effeminate bugler was razzed so badly that he lost his mind and was given a Section 8 discharge. The tense situation with the Welshman came to a sudden end when Lt. Dixon gave the surprising orders that we were to board a train and return to our unit.

"What about our gear?" we complained.

"A black engineering unit is taking it over, and we cannot go aboard and get anything off. You will be issued new gear when you get back."

A couple of months later, we heard that the ship went into Oran, North Africa. There the Germans blew it out of the water, and many of the engineers lost their lives.

Who Gave Who the Crabs at Little Dunmow Near Chelmsford

Little Dunmow was a typical East-Anglian farm village with a pub, post office, greengrocers' and thatched-roofed cottages. The flat pastureland was punctuated with ancient chestnut and beech trees, natural umbrellas for cows and sheep. These great trees also lined the meandering country roads, entwining their limbs overhead and creating long green tunnels. The farmer's fields were defined by hedgerows and board fences, many of them with steep wooden stiles for walkers who wished to take a shortcut.

We were assigned to the Warwick Estate, ten miles outside Chelmsford, to build an airdrome for the 8th Airforce bombers. The main house was taken over by the airforce brass, necessitating that Lady Diane Warwick move into the servant's quarters. A beautiful blonde woman in her late twenties, Lady Diane was married to the Earl of Warwick, who was serving in the Middle East.

She took all of the upheaval of her estate becoming a military camp in good stride, and, on her frequent bicycle trips into Little Dunmow, she kindly picked up a newspaper and delivered it to me where I was operating a bulldozer alongside the lane.

My job was to stockpile cement and aggregate in order to keep the battery of twelve cement mixers going. Bob Tie was still goofing off just as he always did, and this particular morning he was sitting on his ass while everyone else was busting theirs loading the hoppers. When Lt. Dixon showed up and saw Bob doing nothing, he lost his cool, picked up a shovel and threw it at him.

148

"Goddam you, Tie! You get up on that truck and start unloading those sacks of cement," Dixon shouted. "And you don't eat until you are finished."

It was a brutal assignment because English cement bags weigh one hundred twelve pounds, as opposed to American bags which weigh ninety-four, and there were fifteen tons to unload. Nobody sympathized with Tie, however, because he was considered a screw-off who deserved it. Soon thereafter, Tie was given a Section 8 discharge for mental incompetence.

To compensate for the long hard hours of work, a dance was held each week in Chelmsford at the Corn Exchange, a big hall where local farmers sold grain and auctioned livestock. Chelmsford had a large aircraft factory and a huge Marconi wireless plant employing many women. Most of these women came from London and other larger cities and lived full time in the area, so finding a dance and sexual partner was not difficult. But this fraternization, pleasant as it was, often led to other problems.

One afternoon Oakie, Peasley, Gorky, and I were standing around our equipment while Bill, the grease monkey from the airforce, lubricated our machines. We were shooting the breeze about the dance in town, when Oakie piped up, "You know, guys, I've got a case of the crabs."

"Well, it's no disgrace," I said. "Everybody gets the crabs sooner or later."

"Say," Peasley chimed in with his raspy voice akin to Andy Divine's, "I wonder if I ain't got the crabs. I'm itchin'. Do you know what they look like?"

Peasley opened his shirt, exposing a hairy gorilla-like chest that was crawling with hundreds of crabs. We backed away.

"You're alive with crabs, Peasly!" I gasped. "You better get to the medics right away for some blue ointment. I doubt like hell that they've got enough to cover you. You're gonna need a whole bucket of it."

Worse, we knew that Oakie was screwing Joan, the grease-monkey's girlfriend, when Bill was on duty.

"You don't think you gave the crabs to Joan?" I said.

Before Oakie could reply, Bill joined us, lighting up a cigarette. I said, "We missed you yesterday. Did you see Joan on your day off in town?"

"Yeah, I spent the night with her, and I can hardly wait for my next day off. The only problem is, I think I got a case of the crabs,"

Bill complained. "And I don't know where the hell I got 'em."

We weren't about to admit to Bill that we all had crabs, so we didn't say anything except advise him to get some blue ointment. And we never did discover who gave who the crabs.

The Forgotten Bastards

Our engineering regiment of about fourteen hundred men was split up and assigned to different ground and airforce units in England and didn't have a parent organization to fight for it. We came to think of ourselves as "the forgotten bastards." We were sent in small groups to do all the shitty jobs, got the poorest rations, and as soon as we made quarters comfortable, we were moved on. Those following us would enjoy the running water and heated billets while we went ahead to start all over again.

Part of our miserable job at Little Dunmow was to build hangars at various airfields in the Chelmsford area. Eleven of us, including Walt, Tony and I, worked as steel erectors.

The third hangar we constructed was at an airfield near the Henry Ford Estate. Some years earlier Mr. Ford had built an enormous mansion where he had the audacity to keep a garden tractor permanently displayed in the foyer. Combining such commercialism with the gentility of the house and surroundings offended the sensibilities of his neighbors.

Isolated at the airfield, we had to make our own entertainment. On one trip to London, Tony bought a ferret and brought it back to camp so we could hunt rabbits more easily. After work I had been shaking up the stump pile with the bulldozer to scare out any rabbits and run them down. The rabbits would run around the field in circles until they tired. Then they would squat down, and we could easily pick them up. Now, we just set the ferret into the rabbit burrow, and he did the work.

Our latrine here was a shed, with coal scuttles fitted with wooden seats which were used for honey buckets. The two Land Army girls who emptied these every other day were possibly two of the most beautiful women in England.

They drove up in their little black Austin panel truck, emptied the buckets into a tank in the back, washed the receptacles, and replaced the loose-fitting seats. One day, they didn't replace the seat properly on one of the buckets and created a hazardous situation for the unsuspecting user.

Shannon was a big man, well over two hundred pounds, who had recently married an English WAAF twenty years his junior. He was all dressed up and anxious to get going on his twenty-four hour pass to meet his bride of one week when he was caught short and had to use the honey bucket.

Quickly pulling down his pants, he did not notice the position of the seat as he lowered himself, and his pecker fell down between the coal scuttle lip and the seat. Dropping his great weight hurriedly, he trapped and nearly severed his penis. Poor Shannon! The accident prevented him from doing what he had intended to do in the bucket, but, worse, it also prevented him from visiting his bride that evening.

By now, we had been in England for a year and a half, and there was still no sign of going home. We grew more and more depressed every day that passed, and the Friday night dance at the Corn Exchange in Chelmsford was a welcome relief. I drove a six-by-six truck with a load of men on the rec-run to town, parking in front of the dance hall, since we had to be back to the camp before ten o'clock.

The orchestra was playing "The White Cliffs of Dover" as we entered the dimly lit hall. I asked an attractive girl standing by herself if she would like to dance.

"Righto! Ta!" she accepted cheerfully, extending her hand as we moved onto the floor.

"I'm Johnny," I introduced myself.

"And I'm Muriel," she said. "What part of the colonies are you from, Johnny?"

"I'm from the state of Washington—not the capital—the *state* of Washington. It borders on British Columbia, Canada in the Pacific Northwest," I explained knowing that most Britishers thought of D.C. whenever Washington was mentioned. "If you know where that is?"

"I have a vague idea," she said. "I studied Canada in school. It's one of our colonies, you know."

I asked Muriel if she had been taught in school that Britain had lost the Revolutionary War and *the colonies* no longer belonged to Mother England.

She ignored my question. "What did you do in civilian life?" she said, thus avoiding an international incident.

"I worked in the timber industry."

"What is the Pacific Northwest like?"

"It's beautiful and green with lakes, mountains, forests and islands. I live on an island with my wife. Some of the trees are hundreds of years old. They're more than thirteen feet in diameter and over two hundred feet tall," I bragged.

Having learned by now what interested British women, I asked, "Are you familiar with the life cycle of salmon?"

She smiled, "No, I don't have the slightest idea."

"After salmon are hatched in rivers and lakes, they go to sea and stay there until they mature in two to six years, according to the species. They then return to the place where they were born. They have this instinct to return, and regardless of the obstacles in the rivers, they fight their way back. In some cases, the government has built fish ladders to assist them through rapids and dams," I explained.

"I have heard you Yanks tell some fantastic stories," she said, looking at me with disbelieving eyes. "But if you expect me to believe that fish climb ladders—away with you now!"

Before I could defend my story, the whine of air raid sirens put a stop to the dance, and by the time we reached the door, bombs were exploding nearby. It was everyone for themselves, so my new friend Muriel went toward the shelter, and I headed for the truck. Many of the men were already in the back saying, "Let's get going," when a large bomb exploded in a block of houses about six hundred feet away.

Bricks, stone blocks and household furnishings littered the street we had to drive to get back to camp. Fortunately our six-by-six could navigate the rubble, and I was able to make my way without lights to the comparative safety of the two-lane highway to Little Dunmow.

Approaching camp, I noticed tracer bullets piercing the roof of a Niesen hut, sending brief streaks of fire into the night sky.

"What's going on?" I asked Captain Clifford as we both ran toward the open-ended hut.

"Looks like Fender has blown his cork again, and is trying to shoot one of the airplanes down by himself," the captain replied. "I'm going to go in after him, John."

"I'll go with you," I said. Both of us got down on our hands and knees and crawled toward him as he continued firing through the roof.

"Fender," the captain called calmly, "put down your rifle."

To my surprise, Fender handed his piece to the captain and went along to the orderly room without a word. By morning he was gone—on his way home with a Section 8 discharge.

Franco and Guido Court English Land Army Women

Some of the Italian prisoners captured in North Africa had been sent to Wantage, the small village near Oxford where we were assigned to the 9th Airforce. Unlike German POWs, the Italians were not imprisoned, but allowed to travel freely between their billets in the village and the farms where they worked.

Franco and Guido were good-looking young Italians who had sought me out because I spoke their language. Every morning on their way to work, they stopped by to visit. They were disappointed to be in England. They said,"We surrendered to GIs, so why weren't we sent to America?"

"I don't know," I replied, "but you guys have it made here riding around the countryside on bicycles. The war is over for you, but it hasn't really started for us. We still have to go to the continent and win this war."

"Oh, you'll never win this war," Franco said confidently.

"Absolutely not!" Guido said. "As soon as the Allies get to the Piedmont mountains of Northern Italy, you will lose. That will be the end for you."

Since both men were from the Piedmont area, I understood their conviction. Usually, however, our conversation was not about war or politics, but women. We had all been away from home for a long time, and talk often turned to the subject of sex. Perhaps British women were less inhibited than American women or perhaps in England they were just closer to death, but, whatever the reason, they often took pity on the fighting men, and, possibly, on themselves as well. It was as though we clung to each other in desperation, as though holding one another close would make the pain of war go away—at least for a few sweet moments.

So, I listened to Franco and Guido's stories about their beautiful Land Army Girls with considerable pleasure, but I warned them not to get the girls in the *famigilia* way or even get "burnt."

"Don't worry," Franco said proudly. "These girls always bring their own *cappotto* (condom)."

"Italian women never do such a thing," Guido went on. "And these women want it every day!"

"Mine is the most beautiful. *Bella! Bella!*" Franco boasted.

"But mine has the biggest tits. Like a cow." Guido had the last word, illustrating his point by bouncing his open hands up and down below his chest.

A Second Christmas Away From Home

December 1943, and we were still at Wantage—paving roads and constructing a machine shop. Here Mustang fighters were fitted with larger fuel tanks and air scoops to give them greater range as they covered bombers flying into enemy territory. These allied air raids were taking their toll on the Luftwaffe and diminished Germany's ability to bomb England.

This was our second Christmas overseas. With even the invasion of France nowhere in sight, morale was at an all-time low.

In the spirit of the season, we decided to contribute enough money to send a monthly payment to a five-year-old boy whose father had been killed in a London air-raid. Though that bit of holiday generosity made us feel better in one way, it also reminded us that before this goddam thing was over many children would be left fatherless and many wives husbandless back in the States. Nevertheless, the boy and his widowed mother were welcome guests at our Christmas dinner and brightened our day.

"Do you think we'll be home by next Christmas, Johnny?" Captain Colier asked as we finished our coffee.

"Absolutely!" I said. "We will positively be home by next Christmas."

"I'll bet you a hundred bucks we won't," he said dejectedly.

I called his bet and we shook hands on it. I lost the bet, of course, and it was one wager that I'm certain the Captain would have preferred losing himself.

We spent New Year's that year dancing at what we dubbed "the Sweat Box," a small community hall much like our farm granges back in the States. As always, the British and American national anthems were played on the phonograph before the dance records. The Lambeth Walk was very popular at the time, but that evening I was to learn a more exciting dance.

"Coming up next—The Hokey Pokey," the phonograph engineer announced across the room.

A gal grabbed my arm urging, "Come on, Yank! Let's do the Hokey Pokey!"

"But I don't know it," I protested.

154

"Never mind! I'll teach you," she said, rolling her eyes in a teasing way. "Just listen to the words and do as I do."

Put your right hand in
Put your right hand out
Put your right hand in
And roll it all around
You do the hokey pokey
And shake it all around
That's what it's all about.

When the words of the music got to "the back side in and the back side out and roll it all around," every GI in the hall got a dry hump. Of course, the dance was a great hit and since it was new to us, we had to practice it several times before "Auld Lang Syne" was played. In spite of the hilarity of the Hokey Pokey the stroke of midnight turned our thoughts to other New Year's Eves in other places. Kisses mingled with tears as we GIs and our English dance partners remembered lovers and spouses far away.

Getting Close to D Day

Bill and I were chosen to go to Swansea in South Wales to learn how to waterproof motor vehicles so they could operate under water. We were then to go back and teach the rest of our men how to do it. This meant only one thing: the invasion of the continent was getting close, and we would be part of it.

Until then, we made the most of things. In late March, I got an overnight pass to London. The Red Cross Club in Piccadilly was a good place to eat and frequently had lobster for fifty cents. Sometimes, I ordered two meals at a time there. Just around the corner from the club was the Windmill, a theater which had good comedy skits and a nude show. English girls were not allowed to move on stage when nude; instead, they were positioned around the stage in seductive poses. With long, slow droppings of their eyelids, they would signal the audience to survey the rest of their anatomy. Otherwise, each gorgeous woman remained absolutely still as a vocalist sang a popular wartime song, such as "Sentimental Journey" or "The White Cliffs of Dover."

Back at the Red Cross Club, I was having biscuits and coffee when I ran into Walt. We discovered we each had a bunk at the same row house near Hyde Park. About nine o'clock—curfew hour—we were signing in at our sleeping quarters when the air raid sirens went off.

I said, "Let's go and watch the action." Standing in the middle of the street, we saw the searchlight beams swinging back and forth across the sky as the concussion of exploding bombs got stronger and stronger. Then the damndest noise we had ever heard roared out of Hyde Park over our heads. It was a few seconds before we realized that the British had fired all of their rocket propelled anti-aircraft batteries at once, forming a square-mile pattern of flack and, hopefully, bringing down the enemy bombers.

Luckily, the horrendous sound frightened us into the shelter of a doorway. Debris from the exploding rockets fell into the street— one of the three-foot rocket tubes landed exactly where we had been standing. In the morning we read in the paper that seventy-eight people had been trampled to death attempting to get down into the tube for shelter. This was the last major air raid on London. From then on the Germans sent over buzz bombs and V-2 rockets instead.

Shortly after this, our whole unit was sent to Porthcawl, Wales to train in Bailey Bridge construction and V-trestles, used in dock building. This was a grueling exercise that had to be carried on at night in complete darkness. No smoking, no talking, no unnecessary noise at all; we even used rubber hammers. We practiced tasks repeatedly, so we would be able to assemble these structures automatically under the worst conditions.

I designed a collapsible boom for my bulldozer, so that it could also be used as a crane. To build it, I had to steal material from the British Army. The material in their V-trestle was just the ticket. Realizing that most sentries, British and American, didn't know what they were looking at when an identification card was shown to them, I decided to write a trip ticket and pass it off as a legitimate reason for picking up the material.

"Hi mate," I greeted the English guard who stopped Browning and me. "We came to pick up some V-trestle pieces to use in training." He scanned the bogus identification, then motioned us into the sealed-off area. We loaded enough material for a couple of crane booms. As we passed the guard on our way out, we stopped and thanked him.

"Cheerio, mate!" he called back pleasantly.

"Righto, ta," I said.

Next day, we were building the boom when Col. Clifford came by. He said, "John, isn't that V-trestle steel?"

There was no question but that it was, so I said, "Yup, it sure is."

"Where'd you get it?"

"We just went up to the storage site and took it. The guard didn't object at all," I said. "Do you want me to return it?"

"It's all cut up," he said. "You can't return it."

"We're almost finished with it now," I said.

"Go on and complete it, but, John, if you keep on this way, you'll have all of us court martialed."

He left shaking his head in disbelief.

Toward the end of May we began a combat course to prepare for the coming invasion. After breakfast one morning, we started out on a twenty- mile hike. The bivouac area we reached late in the day was a beautiful and quiet Welsh forest. After supper, we laid out our blankets and were preparing for a good night's rest when we heard music coming toward us through the trees. We couldn't believe our ears or our eyes! Our unit chaplain and his assistant, fresh as two daisies, had arrived in a truck with a portable organ.

"Come on, men, we're gonna have a prayer meeting," the chaplain drawled as his assistant played softly in the background.

"Ah, blow it!" Exhausted from our long hike, we weren't about to get up and listen to a holy roller.

"Ah want to impress on you all that you shouldn't be tempted by the ladies of the night," he said. "Too many of you cannot resist the temptation, and you all have families at home to think about. Now, ah want you-all to know that my peckah gets just as hard as yours, and I resist temptation at all times."

Moans of disbelief issued from his congregation. Walt, lying next to me, said, "Listen to that bullshit. That hypocrite usually has a woman on his arm before the convoy stops."

Since no one paid any attention to the pair, they picked up their organ and headed to the truck for their easy ride back. We rolled over in our blankets and tried to sleep, but before our tired backs could get used to the hard ground, the bugler blew reveille, and the sergeants came along and told us to form on the road in twenty minutes.

We did a lot of grumbling, but being good soldiers we also did as we were told. Marching through the night, with short rests for piss call and smokes, we arrived back at camp by mid-morning. I had developed a vericose vein during the forced march, and the calf of my leg felt as if a hot poker was being driven in to it. We all wanted to break ranks and rest, but Lt. Mitchell had other ideas.

"Men, check your bazooka batteries. This is the real thing," he said.

We looked at each other and started laughing. We couldn't

possibly check our bazooka batteries without firing a round that could kill somebody. The embarrassed lieutenant was rattled before he even got into battle.

Again, we were ordered to move out. Just a few hours after our forty-mile hike, exhausted and anxious about what was in store, we loaded the trucks with our GI issue. Since we could take nothing but official equipment along, we gave away our bikes and whatever else we had acquired during our two years in Britain to the Welsh kids and their families. When night came, we stole away.

Browning and I spelled each other driving the truck, and the next day we were back at Wantage speculating just how close D-day was. That night, C-47s pulled gliders overhead. Would our orders come in the morning? But the next day everything was as usual.

It was my day off, and I stopped by the air force repair shop to visit Art who said, "I hear by the grapevine that your outfit is hot."

"Yeah, I'm sure we're close," I said. "This is June, and it would be a good month to go."

"Do you have a sleeping bag?"

"No, we haven't been issued one yet. Our infantry packs are cumbersome as hell just as they are."

"I can get a guy to sew a mummy sack for you out of airplane fabric," Art said. "At least it will keep your blankets off the ground."

The night of June fifth, the gliders were up again, and by ten a.m. next morning the news was out; our troops had landed in France, and we were to follow two days later. Waterproofing our vehicles in case of a wet landing, we were again ordered to get rid of any excess baggage. After supper, the officers brought a keg of beer into our hut. I was asked to dispense it and make sure no one got bent out of shape. The order was quite unnecessary because it was a real solemn beer bust.

I was fairly sure I would never see Doris again because of reports that casualties were high. And though I longed to go back home to my wife and a normal life, I also wanted to participate in the upcoming beach party. I had acquired many engineering skills that could be of invaluable help as our infantry moved toward Berlin, and, besides, I was young and adventuresome.

At twenty-one hundred hours the orderly came in and said our leaving time was changed from four hundred hours to twenty-three hundred hours—within two hours—so we had to forget about sleep.

Browning and I spelled each other driving the Diamond T all night. Between the the hot fumes from the newly waterproofed engine and the acrid smell of our chemically treated long johns and O.D.s (to protect us from anticipated gas attacks), we were both sick by the time we arrived at our marshaling area near Portsmouth. Half-poisoned with chemicals and exhausted from lack of sleep, we were about to begin a war!

9

The Continent At Last

Crossing the Channel and Condoms for All

A little fresh air revived us, and by supper time we were getting hungry. The men who fed us were non-combatant Puerto Rican volunteers, who did nothing but bake and cook for transient troops. Browning and I were parked apart from the others on the side of a black-topped road when a couple of the volunteers arrived in a weapons carrier. They had large kettles of cooked food and huge loaves of white bread, jam and real butter. We asked if we could just have the bread, butter and jam—items we had not seen for the past two years. They were glad to give us anything we wanted, and handed us a large white loaf and the trimmings. Browning, a vegetarian, was even happier with our supper than I was.

After dinner, Browning made himself as comfortable as possible in the seat of the open cab, while I settled down on the canvas between two bows of the truck roof. My mind drifted between thoughts of home and whether or not we would make it on the continent. Suddenly, the skies opened up and drenched us: a third sleepless night!

The next afternoon we removed the fan belts from my bulldozer and Browning's Diamond T, so they could operate underwater if necessary. Now part of the 1st Army, we boarded LST 1087 at Portsmouth. The Navy fed us our "last supper" of creamed chicken and asparagus, something we had not seen since leaving the States.

"Here, get in line ahead of me," I said to the young sailor who was standing nearby. "I have all night to wait, so I'm in no hurry."

"We don't eat that shit," he responded with disdain. "After we dump you guys off on the beach, we will eat steaks."

I was envious: steaks, white bread, and a bunk with sheets. If it wasn't for my chronic motion sickness, I'd have preferred the Navy.

After supper, we were lying on the deck, talking quietly or

160

thinking about what was ahead for us, when the clerk came by with a shoe-box full of condoms.

OK, you guys, take some," he ordered, rather embarrassed.

Al, who apparently wasn't interested in women other than his wife, said, "You've gotta be kidding!"

"Captain's orders," replied the orderly.

"What the hell do we need these for?" Steve said.

"You can pull one over your head and look like a dressed-up hard-on," Al quipped.

"Only a prick like you would recognize one." Steve was not in the mood for jokes.

"Blow it out your ass," Al hollered back.

"Look guys, we're all uptight. Let's knock it off," Lou, the platoon sergeant ordered.

"Ah'll take some." Scotty smiled with anticipation. "Maybe there'll be one of them thar French *madmazoos* on the beach, and I'll get me a piece of French ass," he said in his slow Mississippi drawl.

"This ain't gonna be that kind of a beach party," I said, dampening Scotty's hopes for some strange stuff. "Listen, guys, while I was at waterproofing school, I discovered a great use for rubbers. You can pull one over the end of your rifle barrels to keep it dry. You don't have to worry about taking it off because you can shoot right through it; it won't affect your aim."

I reached into the box for a whole handful of rubbers because I could imagine many uses for them in the field. Taking my watch off, I dropped it into a condom, knotted it, and dropped it into my breast pocket with the end sticking out. For the next three months, all I had to do was pull the safety out and read the time through the sheer latex.

Shortly after dark, we cast off in total blackout, the deck becoming colder and wetter as the night dew settled down upon us. Everything was silent except for the rumble of the slow-turning diesel engine. Like me, everyone was probably thinking of the possibility of getting killed in the next few days.

To break the somber quiet Ed said, "Well, I can just see my wife going down the street with a ten-thousand-dollar insurance check in one hand and a new man on the other." The old joke did not seem very funny that night.

At daybreak our landing craft was in the lead, with another LST about five hundred feet directly behind us. About mid-morning the quiet of anticipation was broken by a heavy explosion muffled by water. The LST off our stern had been struck amidship by a mine rolled into her starboard side by the wake from our boat.

"Do you have any casualties?" our captain hollered through a megaphone.

"There are some," the other commander called back, "but we can handle it. We're taking on water, but believe we can stay afloat."

"The tide will be right to unload in about three hours," our skipper shouted. "Instead of waiting for us to discharge, you come alongside, and we'll beach them together."

Omaha Beach and a Déjà Vu

The day we had anticipated and dreaded for two years was here at last! And it was, after all, an ordinary day. The heavens did not open to reveal the face of God; the skies were not raining fire. Instead, the sun was shining, and the water was calm.

"Is this what we've been getting ready for?" I thought to myself as our LST nosed gently onto Omaha Beach, the Allied code name for this part of the Normandy coast. Off to either side of us were giant steel tripods placed by the Germans to make invasion difficult, but straight ahead our beached bow opened freely to friendly white sand. Eager to be the first one ashore even though it was not a particularly valorous act under the circumstances, I ran down the ramp before anyone else, guiding Browning and his truck off, my bulldozer in tow.

As it turned out, the waterproofing of our vehicles had been completely unnecessary, and we now moved on to a work area to de-waterproof them, ready for land travel. Working quickly through the day, we did not feel like eating our K rations and took only some Nescafe with cold water. Evening found us exhausted, but ahead, though unknown to us, was yet another sleepless night. Right after dark, the Luftwaffe came over, and all hell broke loose. When a battery of 90-MM anti-aircraft guns off to the side of us started firing, the blast lifted us right off the ground.

Flack began falling like rain around us, and a GI who was bent over working on his truck hollered, "I've been hit." Fortunately, he was not wounded badly having taken a piece of falling flack in the cheek of his ass. We led him over to a medics tent across the hedgerow where he was treated and, lucky guy that he was, soon evacuated.

Browning and I caught up with the rest of our unit on the

outskirts of Isigny, about ten miles southwest of Omaha Beach. When we passed through the village, residents waved to us. Everything seemed pretty friendly, except for sniping. A few collaborators had still not been rounded up.

Making camp outside of town, we set up our 20 mm cannon in the middle of a small farmyard. We were spreading the camouflage net over it when an M.E. 109 swooped down. What followed made the Three Stooges look like rank amateurs. Trying to man the gun, our guys became tangled up in the net and fell over one another in their haste. Fortunately, one of our Thunderbolts was right on the Jerry's tail and drove the German plane straight into the drink. The gunners never did get their little cannon to fire, which was OK because I think they would have hit the Thunderbolt.

For the most part, our foxholes were already completed for us thanks to the centuries-old drainage ditches on the perimeter of each field. The most we had to do was a little digging or widening in order to make a space for sleeping for the next three months. On one side of each ditch, hedgerows of hazelnut, willow and other wild

Normandy, July 1944

brush grew out of rocks from the fields that had been stacked into walls about three feet high These walls afforded us protection against enemy fire, but they could be breached with a steady stream of machine gun fire when the infantry needed to get through during an attack.

Sleep was impossible after the air attack. We were too revved up to relax, and when our commander ordered the bugler to sound reveille at daybreak, he played to a wide-awake audience.

General Hodges suddenly appeared from across the lane.

"What in the hell do you think you're doing," he chewed out our commander who stood there dumbfounded. "Don't you know the German line is just fifteen hundred feet up ahead. If you're gonna win this war with a goddam bugle, I'll pull my division out, and you can take over!"

I didn't hear another bugle for the next sixteen months.

Later that morning Browning, Cramoga and I were sent back to Omaha Beach to clear away the remaining steel tripods and mines. We had barely started when Captain Dixon came and told us to go to Carantan—ten miles away—and fill bomb craters so the tanks could get through.

"Captain," I objected, "we heard that Carantan was lost again during the night.

"Well, I don't know anything about that. I just know what our time schedule says, and that means you go to Carantan and fill craters," he said. "I'll catch up with you guys later this afternoon."

We drove off, map in hand, trailing the dozer behind the truck. About five miles down the road, we arrived at the town square of Formigny and were baffled as to which of the several roads radiating from it led to Carantan. There were no signs, but in the very center of the square stood a large wooden cross draped with both German and American communications wires. I was stunned as I stood before it. Somehow, somewhere I had seen this place and this cross before. Perhaps the stress and tension we were under had thrown me into an altered state of consciousness, or, perhaps, I had had a precognitive dream, but whatever the déjà vu was, I knew this place. I knew beyond any doubt which road led to Carantan.

Behind Enemy Lines

At the Carantan bridge an MP waved us to a stop then took shelter next to a high stone wall. Uncannily, within seconds an 88 shell exploded just ahead of us, hitting a pontoon bridge and sinking it—leaving the single Bailey bridge for access between the two beach-heads.

"How in the hell did you know that was coming?" I said

"Just stand here quietly," he said, "and you'll see."

In a few minutes we felt the earth shaking, and the MP said, "Get behind the wall—we've got seven or eight seconds!"

It turned out that this guy controlled traffic by hearing or actually feeling the concussion when the Germans fired one of their many 88's at the bridge and knowing how long it took the shell to arrive. At that point I gained a lot of respect for combat MPs. That had to be one of the most nerve-wracking jobs in the army.

Between shells, we crossed over into Carantan and got our first view of death and destruction up close. A couple of Frenchmen were throwing dirt on the bodies of two dead American paratroopers. Nearby, the dead GIs rifles had been stuck into the ground and their helmets placed on top. As we stared in sadness at the scene, the Frenchmen acknowledged four dead comrades, and then casually asked us for cigarettes. They each took two: one they lit up and the other was stuck behind their ear for later.

A couple of blocks up ahead we saw the airborne in a skirmish line. Their medics had armed themselves in retaliation for the Germans firing at men with medic armbands. The GIs spread out to let us through, and a short distance further we found ourselves in the middle of enemy fire. We jumped out of the truck into a hole near the church, and I worked my way back on foot to the paratroopers.

"What's going on here?" I said, more than a little pissed off.

"The Germans are all over the place! That's what's going on up here," one GI said.

"We were told that you guys had taken Carantan."

"Well, we did yesterday We lost it during the night."

"What in the hell did you let us go through for?"

"We thought you were going to win the war all by yourself," a wise ass responded.

There was nothing to do but return to Browning and Cramoga, and figure a way to get our equipment out from behind enemy lines. Unable to turn around in the narrow old streets, we decided to go on through town. A Frenchman pushing a cartload of dead civilians got in the way. In desperation we hollered to him, motioning him off the street, and continued on, bearing left as we worked our way back to our line. Cramoga and I fired steadily from the cab as Browning drove us down what seemed the unending half mile of French street. Miraculously, we got ourselves and our equipment safely back over the bridge where we awaited the arrival of Captain Dixon.

I blew my stack when he showed up. "We were behind enemy lines!"

He said without apology, "Sorry, I had bad information."

After about five hours, the three of us crossed the bridge into Carantan once again, this time accompanied by the captain and his driver. I set to work filling the bomb craters with my dozer as Cramoga covered me against incoming enemy fire. It was unnerving as hell to see a building, not one hundred feet away, hit by an 88 and come crumbling down.

Carantan was a vital point for both sides. The only road connecting Omaha Beach and Utah Beach, directly across the bay, ran through Carantan. Whoever controlled that road controlled the strategic Cotentin Peninsula of Normandy. So, after spending the night back at Isigny, we returned to the village to fill shell craters down by the railroad station. I had barely got started when the Germans zeroed in on us again, and an 88 exploded on the bank above showering us with dirt.

When an ME-109 came down the track strafing us, we dove into a bomb crater near some airborne who had dug in. When things calmed down, a couple of the paratroopers came over and shared a bottle of Calvados with us.

This was France, after all, so there was plenty of liquor available. As it turned out, our lieutenant dealt with the pressure and constant shelling by escaping into the bottle. Constantly drunk, he left us to deal with the situation as best we could. Still a small unit with no parent outfit, we felt more than ever like "the forgotten bastards."

Since our prime objective was to open the roads and repair the railroad to Cherbourg on the northwestern coast of the peninsula, Lou, Al and I moved out to see what needed to be done about a railroad bridge that the Germans had blown up. As soon as we got there, Germans opened fire from behind us. With no cover nearby, we flattened out on the ground as the slugs hit the dirt three feet from my face. We figured the Jerries were too nervous to take good aim, because when we decided to run a couple of hundred feet for cover, we were not hit. About that time a squad of newly arrived infantry swept in and cleaned the Germans out of the houses where they were holed up under the protection of French collaborators.

As the battle for control of Carantan continued to rage, a terrible storm blew up in the Channel and made it impossible for the Allies to land supplies or armor. When we asked why more Allied shots were not being fired at the Jerries, we were told the airborne was almost out of ammunition. They were limited to one 75 mm Howitzer round a day. "One shot a day! How can we win a war this way?" we despaired. If the Germans had counter attacked at this point, they surely could have pushed us back into the drink.

Grim as the situation was, it was not without its humor. Or perhaps it would be more accurate to say that under great stress we found laughter was the only way to deal with situations that in other circumstances would have seemed repulsive. We had just arrived at the work site when a Messerschmit-109 flew low overhead, strafing us. Everyone but a guy by the name of Stookey took cover behind a stone wall. Stookey flattened out in the garden which, unknown to him, the Jerries had used for a toilet. Hagen, who was with us behind the wall, started shooting at the ME-109 and as the spent cartridges flew out of his M-1, they hit Stookey in the back. Stookey was sure he was being hit by slugs and buried his face deeper and deeper into the crap. When it was over, he stood up dripping with shit, and we all laughed until we cried.

Cooking German Rations, July 1944

Everyone had only one change of clothes, and since Stookey had
no alternative but to change, we decided to follow suit. Our chemically treated underwear had smelled more sickening with every
passing day. As we discarded it, we just hoped the Germans wouldn't
use gas.

Vignettes on the Way to Cherbourg and a Russian Chorus by Night

As the battle for the Cotentin Peninsula continued, two platoons of
our company were ordered to move on to the port of Cherbourg at
the head of the peninsula. Signs of battle were everywhere as we
wound our way through the devastated countryside. St. Mère Eglise
was shattered and crumbled; Montebourg was burning on both sides
of the road.

We stopped at Valognes where we were to secure the railroad
station before continuing to Cherbourg. The infantry was already
dug in when we arrived, so all we had to do was take up our positions.
Scotty, the Mississippi Don Juan, hadn't found his "Madmazoo" yet,
but he soon discovered a basement under a cafe near the station that
was full of assorted wines and liquors, and shared his prizes generously. By the time the shelling started, Torgerson was passed out
under the stairway, so drunk that when plaster fell on him, he didn't
even rouse. About that time a battalion of tanks came by to support
the advancing infantry, and as they passed us, we handed each
tanker five or six bottles of spoils to buoy up their spirits.

A short while later, Al, Lou, and I got into the railroad office and
found a whole safe full of paper money. The decision was made that
I would take all of it, and we would divide it later. Throwing my gas
mask away, I filled the carrier with bills and put the rest in my
raincoat pockets.

That afternoon a Frenchman came up to me with his daughter.
I had learned that my facility with Italian made it possible for me to
understand French, and I had no trouble comprehending him as he
told me that two GIs had raped his fifteen-year-old daughter while
he stood by helpless. He wanted me to find the men who had held
him at gunpoint while they took turns raping his daughter. There
was really nothing I could do but tell Lt. Mitchel, who simply
shrugged his shoulders. Such things happen in wartime.

We moved into Cherbourg with the infantry and bivouacked on
Tourlaville Hill overlooking the harbor. Thousands of Germans who
had surrendered in Normandy were kept next to us behind a huge

and hastily-built barbed wire enclosure. Among them were about five thousand Russians from the Georgian area, whom the Germans had captured and brought to the coast to build Hitler's west wall.

At night the Russians sang, their great chorus filling the evening air with what we could only imagine were sad love songs and melancholy longings for home. The sonorous beauty of their voices raised us temporarily above and beyond the ugliness of war.

Cherbourg

The Germans had completely demolished the port of Cherbourg, blowing up all possible moorings in the inner harbor, as well as loading small boats with concrete and sinking them in the locks to render them useless.

The morning that Walt and I decided to go into one of the huge pillboxes and look around, we were aware of what we had come to call "the war cloud" hanging overhead. For days we had noticed that, when a bitter battle had taken place, there would be a dark cloud directly above the area. Maybe there was scientific explanation for it involving the chemicals and heavy bombardment of war.

As we entered the pillbox that morning, the cloud hovering ominously overhead opened and poured down a deluge of water. The pillbox turret had taken a direct hit, and we could still feel the heat from the flame throwers. Walt was ahead of me as we started up the stairs which, by now, were flowing with rain as well as blood. When he reached the landing where the machine guns rested mute in their slits, he called back to me, "Do you want a glove for a souvenir, Johnny?"

Before I could respond, he handed me a glove with a severed hand in it. "Walt, you bastard," I muttered as I dropped it. "Those guys are all dead and I feel sick." I barely made it outside to fresh air.

I was assigned to help the navy mine experts uncover large sea mines that hadn't exploded when the enemy demolished the huge masonry and steel dock with its beautiful copper roof. I had been told there was really very little danger. Well, that was true to a point. As I was dragging the first mine out of the rubble as gently as possible with my bulldozer, I suddenly realized all the rest of the demolition team and the photographers had retreated to a safe distance.

I worked all day dragging the mines out of the rubble, and in the end I was the only one who didn't get a medal for doing a job under hazardous conditions. Our lieutenant, who would have been the one to recommend me for the commendation, was off looking for alcohol.

After our evening meal of K-rations, Walt and I decided to walk down the tree-lined road to a small cafe for a drink ourselves. We carried our rifles slung over our shoulders because there were still a few hold-outs around harassing us with sniper fire. The room was very small, apparently part of the proprietor's home, and just large enough for two tables with chairs and a shelf that served as bar. Gromaski, one of our men who was drunk and leaning against the bar, grabbed at the pre-teen daughter of the owner as she passed to take the orders of four GIs sitting at one of the tables.

Walt and I ordered a glass of wine each, and watched the kid as she went back to the bar. Again the drunk Gromaski grabbed the little girl by her ass and tried to kiss her. Walt and I were ashamed and disgusted, but the kid's parents didn't seem to object to his advances. The little waitress brought us our wine, which we paid for with our invasion money—the first chance we'd had to spend any of it.

At the table the two paratroopers and the two infantry men were getting louder and louder in their argument over who had contributed more to the success of the campaign, the airborne or the infantry. All four were pretty well oiled and got more and more abusive as the argument heated up. Here we were, seven armed GIs in a room not more than twelve feet square, and we decided it was time to get out. Quickly downing our wine, we left the arguers with Gromaski and the French family.

About three hundred feet up the road, we heard a shot from the cafe and knew the best thing we could do was get back to camp. An hour or so later, our battalion adjutant led a staggering Gromaski to his fox hole admonishing him not leave the area for any reason.

It was two days before Walt, Gromaski and I were called, one at a time, before a court martial board and learned that one of the paratroopers had shot and killed one of the infantrymen.

We Divide Our Spoils of War

It was the first time Lou, Al and I had gotten together since we found the money back at Valognes. I was tired of carrying it around, and we went down into one of the big pillboxes to divide our spoils. Just outside the entrance, a jeep passed us with a half dozen dead GIs piled on the back, arms and legs hanging askew. Once inside, we sat down on the steps, and peering down into the darkness, we could just barely make out two Germans lying face down in a few inches of water. Not even this grizzly sight deterred us from our self-serving assignment.

Because we had so much money, we decided to throw all the two-franc notes (worth about five cents), down the stairs, where they floated around among the dead enemy. We were almost finished sharing our bounty, when a couple of quartermaster GIs looked in and asked if there were any dead men down there.

"There's at least two," Al said.

When the men spotted the money, they forgot all about the corpses in their watery grave and began splashing around among the dead gathering up bills and shouting with glee. War hardened all of us.

We ended up with more than two hundred dollars apiece. We were unable to send money home, but we could buy money orders made out to ourselves. I saved one hundred dollars of my money just in case I lost my bet to Colyer that we would be home by next Christmas. At this point, it looked as though he was going to win.

The General Gets a Medal and Jack Gets a Strange Creature on His Peter

Soon after we advanced into Cherbourg, the general commanding the Corps of Engineers came to inspect his troops, and there was a ceremony on the back of a truck bed. We were called together to see him receive a medal for being exposed to the enemy above and beyond the call of duty. No matter that most of us had gotten there three days before him: we didn't get a diddly shit.

Jack Doyle, however, got something—albeit, not a medal. Jack, Walt and I were sent to the beautiful estate owned by a French general on the northeast point of the peninsula. Near the town of Barfleur, the estate was set deep in the woods at the end of a winding lane. We were to cut trees to be used for dock piling.

One afternoon, Jack came to Walt and me after taking a piss, looking painfully worried.

"Hey guys, I got something wrong with my pecker, and I don't know what the hell it is," he said.

"The hell you have." We were afraid he might have contracted a horrible disease. "Let's have a look."

Embedded on the end of his circumcised peter was the biggest, fattest wood tick I had ever seen. How it ever could have burrowed into him without Jack's knowledge, I never understood—until years

171

later when I learned that ticks emit an anesthetic as they dig in. The scene seemed hilariously funny, as I realized that anybody seeing Walt and me inspecting Jack's pecker would wonder what in the hell was going on.

"Better not try to pull him out," I advised. "He's dug in deep."

By then, Walt and I were laughing ourselves sick, but poor old Jack couldn't see the humor. It was, after all, his body part that was ailing.

"What am I going to do," he said.

"Why don't you shake it a couple of times?" I suggested. "Maybe you can shoot the little bastard off."

In the end we took him over to airforce headquarters, where a medic took a look at it. We gave the medic all the advice we could, suggesting that he could possibly cut a piece off the end of Jack's penis. Poor Jack was anguished when the medic left, presumably to get a scalpel and scissors. When he returned with a tweezer, we decided we had better knock off the shit because Jack had gone through enough. We watched fairly sober-faced as the medic lit a cigarette and put the hot end to the all-but-exploding body of the tick. The blood-filled creature relaxed his grip at once, and the medic deftly pulled him out. We always thought Jack should have gotten a medal for bravery above and beyond the call of duty.

Walt Finds Two Medallions

We had just loaded the trailer with logs and were waiting for Browning to return when we decided to explore the general's chateau. It had been used by the upper echelon Wermacht, so we knew we had better be careful; they always left left thousands of anti-personnel bombs scattered wherever they had been. These were small devices that looked much like a Carter's Little Liver Pills can, and, sure enough, they were lying around all over the grounds and among anything that we might want as a souvenir.

The house was filled with treasures that included the largest and most ornate grand piano I have ever seen. In the basement we found many large chests filled with sterling silver flatware. Regretfully, we realized we probably could not get it home. When Walt reached into one of the chests, he came up with two gold medallions, each at least a quarter of an inch thick by three inches in diameter, and those prizes he could easily carry on his person.

By then, I was pretty fluent in French and translated the

172

inscription for him. Ironically, the medals had been awarded in the 1800s to a baroness for her support of the aristocracy during one of the French revolutions.

An Insult and an Understanding

Our unit was assembling a row of stiff legs on a long concrete dock, so barges of materials could be tied up and unloaded. On one of our occasional days off, I decided to go down the hill into Cherbourg to look at the damage. Finding a small cafe serving food, I joined two airborne lieutenants at their invitation because there were no other tables available. A few minutes later Stevens came in, drunk as hell. He took the only chair he could find—the one remaining at our table.

"How the hell are all you Dagos making it?" he asked, looking at me and slurring his words as he spoke.

"Just fine," I said, not wanting to make a scene.

The two officers saw my anger and were also embarrassed by this uninvited drunk who was ruining dinner for all of us. Without finishing our eggs and fried potatoes, the three of us left. My parting words to Stevens were, "I'll see you in camp."

The more I thought about it, the madder I got, but I wanted to be sure he was sober when I talked to him. The following morning I picked up my M-1, and confronted him as he sat on the edge of his foxhole.

"Steve, if you ever mention one more word about Dagos, I'll blow your fucking head off," I said, holding the barrel of my rifle to his head. "You're sober now, and I just want to be sure you understand what I'm saying."

"I didn't mean you," he whimpered. "I meant all of the others."

"Well, I mean it for all of us."

He never mentioned Dagos again—at least, not in front of me. Perhaps that was the last time I reacted so angrily to negative comments about my Italian heritage. As the war dragged on, I grew more confident of my abilities and less sensitive to what others thought of me. In the tangle of death and violence we know as war, I was growing as a human being.

The morning I slipped out of my foxhole bedroll to find a make-shift cross with a dog-tag and a sign announcing "Dago John R.I.P.," I was able to laugh for the first time at a taunt about my background.

When a shipping crate became my apartment, I actually enjoyed the sign "Dago John's Place" put up by some of the guys. I was beginning to like Dago John more and more.

Saturday is Hanging Day

"Hangman wanted. Tech-sergeant rating. Preferably experienced," the communique said. I understood the meaning of that advertisement, signed by General Eisenhower, more fully the day we moved into the Cherbourg navy yard to raise a scuttled German ship. There on the dock was a structure that looked like a hangman's scaffold. However, we didn't fully understand what was going on until a day later, when another scaffold was erected.

Walt asked, "Do you want to watch the hangings on Saturday?"

"No thanks," I said. "I've seen enough dying."

Sergeant George Brown

Sergeant George Brown was one of the best soldiers in our unit. He had done a hitch in peacetime, and volunteered for this one. He was single and loved soldiering, being especially good at deactivating mines and booby traps. The Germans had taken a lot of pains to booby-trap a fine old house at a strategic point on the channel. They had buried Teller mines in the concrete driveway, covering them with a thin layer of cement so they would not be detected.

Fortunately, we discovered this maze of booby traps with our mine detectors. Dogface Brown, as we affectionately nicknamed him, volunteered to disarm them. This extremely hazardous task accomplished, he went on into the house, where even the wooden stair treads had to be deactivated. In all, he removed one hundred thirty-eight traps.

The St. Lô Breakthrough, Rebuilding the Power Line and Mire Around the Nurses Tents

It was important for the Allies to take St. Lô in their strategy to cut across the peninsula and fan out, securing the Brittany peninsula and entrapping the Germans. Cherbourg was about twenty miles from St. Lô, but at five o'clock on a morning in late July we could feel the ground rumble as our heavy bombers circled overhead, waiting their turn to drop their deadly cargo on the German-held French village. That day twenty-four hundred sorties were flown, with some planes returning to England for a second load. Every available artillery piece fired until dark, and the famous St. Lô breakthrough was successful.

The price was high, however. Smoke markers were dropped in the wrong places, and some of our planes mistakenly killed our own men. After this, the battleship *Texas* was brought into Cherbourg to be used as a power generator and tie into the land grid while we were assigned to rebuild the power transmission line to St. Lô. The line ran directly through an area where many GIs died, and when Buorkman, one of our unit, was questioned as to where he got the American money he was drying on strings in our bivouac area at Pont Hebert, he admitted to a ghoulish routine. Whenever he came upon dead soldiers, he went through their pockets.

As we strung cable across a valley, we discovered many German bodies in a small stream that was the source of our drinking water. Fortunately for us, our water purification unit was treating all drinking and cooking water; it was easier to remove the dead than to find a new source of water.

Replacement of the towers was well underway. Ed was a steeple-jack back in the States and felt right at home in a bos'n chair. Tony was good at steel work, and Walt was just plain versatile. We just decided among ourselves what each would do and then did it.

One day we were pulling the slack out of the war-weary cable when it broke. I was inside one of the steel towers sighting the sag in the line as three of the towers folded like dominoes toward me. The tower I was in folded about ten feet above my head, and I climbed down unhurt, but more hesitant than ever about steel work.

The power line was finally completed, and we were in a rest pattern, until a field evacuation hospital fresh from the States moved into the outskirts of Isigny. Now, we began working around the clock to build a surgery. I pulled night shift, and was therefore able to practice my French with local people during the day. Young children, like Maxim and Leona, were most helpful because their vocabulary was simple, and they were patient. I didn't realize how hungry the kids were until I saw them pick food out of our garbage cans. Then I talked to Captain Dixon about giving them our untouched leftovers, for which they were very grateful. Remembering my hunger when I was a kid in Brooklyn, I was glad to be able to help these kids and their families. And I was coming to recognize the common humanity of people beyond the anonymity of the uniform and the nameless face. When a convoy of badly wounded prisoners was brought in and laid in rows on the floor of a receiving tent, many of them begged us for cigarettes. We were forbidden to associate in any way with these men, but knowing that they were suffering terrible pain and would probably die, we learned to overcome the rules. In our growing compassion, we would light cigarettes and drop them on the floor near their litters so they could pick them up.

Everything suffers in war, even innocent animals like the little white goat I named "Nanette." She lost her left hind leg below the knee to a mine, and had learned to get around using a jumping and bouncing movement. Every day she would appear at my tent, and I fed her peanuts and worried that she would step on another mine and be killed.

The surgical hut was progressing nicely, but winter was coming on and the nurses' tents were all but adrift in mud. We helped out by recycling their wooden packing crates,using them for sidewalks, floors and side walls. The nurses were not allowed to socialize with GIs, but they showed their appreciation by giving us all of their liquor rations.

Paris is Liberated and Walt Disappears

After much bloody fighting, Paris was finally liberated. It was DeGaulle's day, and GIs were not permitted to enter the city until the Free French Forces had led the way. We were angry because we wanted to see the fabled City of Light that we had helped to liberate.

I was called into the orderly tent one morning, and Captain Dixon asked if I knew where Walt was.

He said, "He's been missing since yesterday,"

"Maybe he's been blown up by a mine." Walt was an avid trophy scavenger. "Or maybe he bummed a ride to Paris."

"Do you think he'd go when he knows it's off limits?"

"I sure as hell do. We're this close and we can't go. I wouldn't blame him if he did. I know he's not interested in women, but he wants to see the sights."

"That's all, John," the captain said. "I just hope he isn't dead."

Walt showed up about 3 o'clock that afternoon. He never revealed where he had been, and nothing was done about it because he was a very good and dedicated soldier. I think Walt simply did what the rest of us wanted to do.

Clearing Mines Near Valenciennes, Enjoying a French Greeting and Becoming Infantrymen

We were sent on to Valenciennes, near the Belgian border, to clear mines at a Luftwaffe airfield, a nerve-wracking detail. Winter was closing in, and every day I could see my hundred-buck bet that we would be home by Christmas slipping away to Captain Colyer. Those of us who were able-bodied were alerted to move on to the Battle of the Bulge. Disabled and older men were left behind to guard our equipment.

A quartermaster outfit picked us up, and we rode all day and night huddled together for warmth in the open vehicles. At daybreak when we stopped to refuel the trucks and eat our cold K rations, we saw a greeting between a Frenchman and a Frenchwoman that sent us into gales of laughter. Parked in front of two farms separated by a barbed wire fence, we watched as the gentleman farmer and his neighbor walked toward us through their respective fields. Apparently they were going to see what was going on with our parked trucks, but, first, they would greet each other.

The man got to the fence first, and as he waited for the woman, he unbuttoned his pants and began to piss. She continued to approach cheerfully, offering her hand to him across the fence when she arrived. He reached out with his left hand since his right hand was busy, never once slowing down the stream of pee that hit the ground near their feet. They shook hands heartily, obviously very glad to see each other.

"*Bon Jour, Madame, Bon Jour, Monsieur,*" I called out to them, not able to resist becoming part of what was to us a delightfully funny scene.

"*Bon Jour, Bon Jour,*" they both replied, smiling back at us.

We were more than smiling; we were hysterical.

"Help him out, Madame," Ed hollered brashly in English.

I'm sure they did not understand our amusement, but they laughed along with us.

That small interlude helped us through the rest of the day. By dark we had arrived at the Meuse River, and were split up into two groups. I was sent to a large room in a two-story building with about fifty others. As we stretched out on the floor to sleep, whole families of refugees traipsed around us into adjoining rooms.

Before morning we learned that the Germans had broken through our lines, and we were to take up defensive positions on the other side of the Meuse River west of Bastogne. We were now infantrymen!

Two hundred Free French guerillas came up to reinforce us. Dressed in all sorts of ragtag clothing, the only items they had in common were berets and automatic weapons.

As we patrolled in the bitter cold, our C-rations and the water in our canteens froze—even though we carried them close to our bodies. But we were sometimes frozen in fear as well as we crossed the Meuse River into no-man's land, tracer bullets streaking the sky overhead in both directions. Our concern was not only the Germans but also the trigger-happy guerillas who were liable to pop out from behind a tree or rock and shoot us in error. The Luftwaffe knew where we were, and every night during the bright of the moon a German pilot flying a Junker 88 would swoop down and strafe us. We dubbed him "Bed Check Charlie," and when the moon darkened, he no longer came. Some weeks later, when Browning returned to our unit after being hospitalized, he reported that "Bed Check Charlie" had been shot down and was a patient in the bed next to him.

Before we knew it, Christmas had come again, and I had lost my hundred-dollar bet to Captain Colyer. But I felt a little better when General Eisenhower announced that every GI in the European theater would have a turkey dinner. However, to the dismay of our cooks, the four birds that arrived had been chewed by rats. The chefs trimmed the ragged edges and made arrangements with the local baker to roast them in exchange for some GI rations.

As our Christmas dinner was roasting, two Belgian nuns appeared at our living quarters and invited us to a special service to be held by the village priest.

"I'm not going," I said. "I would feel like a hypocrite because I'm not a religious person."

"Come on, John. If the priest is going to the trouble of a special service for us, we should go," Al said.

"It won't hurt you, John. Just come along," Lou said.

I gave in and followed them to the church on the stipulation that we would all pray only one prayer—that our planes would come through and stop the Germans.

As we crossed the street under low gray skies, the town crier rang his bell announcing the special Christmas service, but no one entered the small stone church except we four GIs and three nuns in their white-winged hats. The church was dark except for a few flickering candles and the dim light from recessed windows. Kneeling down, we prayed our prayers for the planes to get through—at least I did, and I hoped the others were keeping their promise.

Ten minutes into the service, we heard the drone of bombers in the distance. My heart flickered like the candles at the altar, and I tilted my head and listened. For a moment I was in harmony with something mysterious in the universe—as though I was certain I would get through this war alive, as though the planes would get through. The experience was like that at Formigny, where I knew beyond ordinary, everyday knowing which road to take.

Hours later, we learned our planes had been able to drop their bombs on the enemy through an unexpected opening in the clouds at the very time we were praying. By then the wonder of the feeling of oneness with some intent in the universe had passed, and I was back to analyzing with my twentieth-century scientific mind. It had to be coincidence that the clouds opened at that precise time on that particular Christmas Day. Clouds don't respond to prayer! Nevertheless, it is an experience I have never forgotten.

More Fighting, Cold and Sickness

As the winter wore on, the cold became even more brutal and so did our feelings toward any soldier who shirked his duty. When a soldier did not show up to relieve his man at the forward observation post, he wasn't just AWOL, he was considered a deserter. Captain Dixon wanted the twenty-year-old who failed to show up on time executed on the spot, but other officers intervened at the court martial hearing, and he was given five years—a high price to pay for a night in bed with a local *mademoiselle*.

The Germans were dropping paratroopers behind our lines. We would barely lie down to rest, having patrolled all night, when we would be sent out to hunt the enemy. Frightened, exhausted and suspicious, I nearly shot two of our own men who did not heed my warning to halt as they approached on a motorcycle. The driver, a Canadian paratrooper wearing his helmet—much like a German helmet—and a friend of mine riding double behind him, did not stop until I drew a bead, and they realized I meant business. The Canadians were laying mines in the area, and the guy driving the bike was coming in to borrow an air compressor to drill the frozen ground.

Perpetually cold and fatigued, we were beginning to fall ill. The morning the order came out that no soldier could report for sick call if he was ambulatory, I found Lou lying on the floor of his quarters.

"The Captain says you are to take a detail across the river," I said, kneeling down beside Lou where he lay bundled up in his blankets.

"I'm sick, Johnny. I'm too sick to go," Lou said, shivering noticeably under his covers.

When I reported back to Captain Dixon he retorted, "What the hell's the difference if he dies here or on the other side of the river?"

Perhaps it was rage at the heartless response that gave Lou the wherewithal to to pick himself up from the floor. Whatever it was, Lou did as he was ordered, vowing to kill the captain. "If that son-of-a-bitch comes across the river, I guarantee he won't come back alive."

A few days later we were relieved by the 17th Airborne division from Britain where they had been training for the Rhine River crossing. The German breakthrough changed these plans and gave them a taste of battle sooner than they expected. On occasion we would encounter some of these troopers, also on patrol. One night I spotted a man in the darkness, and not knowing if he was a GI or not, I stuck my rifle barrel in his stomach and gave the password for the day. At the same time he stuck an automatic weapon in my belly.

"Clara," I spit out at him.

"Bow," he answered instantly, as happy as I that we had not shot each other.

We were now in Belgium. I had been ill for two days, but managed to keep going. On our way to Antwerp in the northeast, I asked the driver to stop so I could check into a hospital at La-Louviere where the medical corps had set up shop in a university.

"You are a sick man," the medic said as he shook his head at my temperature of 105 degrees. "We'll get you into bed right away."

I not only had pneumonia, but I developed strep throat as well. Fortunately, sulfa and penicillin were available and when I began to feel better after a week or so, I learned I had been close to death.

"Hi, soldier! " a pretty young nurse said one evening. "Your doctors thought they were going to lose you." She felt my forehead, "but you're gonna make it now for sure."

For the first time I noticed that she was wearing a purple heart. She had been awarded it for her work at the Anzio Beachhead.

"We were under constant fire there," she said, "and just about everyone in our hospital unit was wounded at one time or another."

Another sign that I was getting better that night was that I noticed how attractive she was.

I said, "You are a living image of Joan Crawford."

She smiled, "I've been told that before."

From that time on, I called her "Joan," never mind that she was a lieutenant and could have pulled rank on me. She was obviously different from the lieutenant who was later admitted with a cold. Given a bed at the end of my row, he immediately began complaining about his lack of privacy.

After a few hours of his hell-raising, the nurses hung blankets from the ceiling to partition him off.

"I guess he doesn't think he should be in a ward with us dogfaces," I said.

"We treat everyone the same," my nurse said. "Rank doesn't get special privilege here."

A couple of weeks later, I was astonished to see Captain Dixon standing beside my bed.

"Are you sick, too?" I queried, unable to accept that he would take time to visit me.

"No, I'm not sick. This is the first chance I've had to catch up with you. I just wanted to know how you are doing," he replied, handing me my mail and a carton of cigarettes.

Buzz Bomb Alley

After five weeks of bed rest, I joined my unit in Antwerp, a little weak but happy to join up with the old gang. A couple of the guys were gone, having cracked up with the strain of working under shellfire, strafing and bombing. Those stresses, coupled with having been overseas for nearly two and one-half years, were beginning to take their toll.

Antwerp was known as buzz bomb alley: you could see and hear the bombs coming for a couple of miles. They looked like small fighter planes, hurtling toward us six or seven hundred feet above the ground. Since they were set to explode on impact, we had to sweat them out until they were overhead and still going. To make matters worse, Axis Sally beamed her American music to us, and her predictions of just when we could expect another buzz bomb were always accurate. Just as demoralizing, she knew our unit number and location.

An article in *Yank* magazine dubbed our engineering unit the "Gypsy Builders," because we moved quickly from one project to another, often stealing away in the dead of night.

"When an engineer outfit moves in, it does things in a big

way...and moves on. It leaves behind water towers, and warehouses and hangars, mess halls, Nissen huts, concrete walks—wiring, plumbing, piping.

These engineers don't build Boulder Dams—nothing fancy, no miracles, but only the necessary homely items of construction by which an Army lives. When they are through they fold the heavy machinery and steal off—and the Army moves in the next day."

One of our big jobs at Antwerp was cleaning up the debris of a movie theater that had taken a direct hit by a buzz bomb, which killed fifteen GIs. Immediately afterwards we were sent to Herstal, on the outskirts of Liegè on the eastern Belgian-German border. Here we were bivouacked in a comfortable brick schoolhouse. At nearby Neuville we were to complete a chapel at an American cemetery used to accommodate the overflow from Henri Chapel near the German border. The location of the cemetery was an old estate with tall poplar trees lining the narrow dirt lane leading to the new graves where Christian and Jewish GIs were laid to rest side by side. These graves gave me the feeling that part of me would be staying here: we had all fought for the same cause.

When the chapel was complete, a Christian cross was placed on the steeple. We thought we were finished, but a couple of days later, we were ordered to remove the cross and replace it with the star of David. That symbol was subsequently ordered removed, also. This continued for a couple of weeks, with every possible combination of symbols being tried. When I finally came off that job, the steeple was bare—which made it non-denominational.

And again, I was to move on. This time alone! No other member of my unit was to go with me.

"Base section headquarters needs someone who speaks French and drives a truck. You fill the bill, so you are to report to Lt. Col. Bianco in the morning for your orders," Captain Dixon said.

I looked forward to the assignment, sensing that some intrigue was involved. To whom would I be speaking French? Where and why would I be driving a truck?

10

Eighteen Carloads of Silver and the End of the War

The Furniture Factory and Madame Savoie

Reporting to Colonel Bianco, I found myself in a luxurious home that had been commandeered for American officers. When I arrived, I was shown to the basement, now a kitchen and dining room for the unit officers assigned there. Attractive Belgian women were serving breakfast, and as they poured coffee, they gave a peck on the cheek to each man. Certain favorites had even warmer kisses bestowed on them. I was surprised that the officers lived in such luxury, apparently being served food and sex by the same charming women. The thought ran through my mind that they probably never had experienced this type of high living in the States.

After breakfast Colonel Bianco took me to his office and gave me orders to report to the Givet Furniture Factory for any duties that were required. Monsieur Savoie, the owner, did not speak much English, so I was introduced to his son Marcel and told that he would be my civilian counterpart. The furniture factory had been demolished by a buzz-bomb attack. Our main job was to get it back on line.

Monsieur Savoie was natty in a dark business suit and Hambourg. Since his factory was large, he was undoubtedly wealthy, and his speech and manners showed he was well-bred. Marcel was also dressed in a smart suit—obviously well-educated and upper class.

The first day Marcel and I went to pick up a load of cement at a little village outside Liegè. About noon, we stopped at a roadside cafe for a lunch that turned out to be black market eggs, fried potatoes and a Belgian endive salad.

After the meal we sat enjoying a last glass of wine when Marcel asked pleasantly in his Belgian-French, "Would you like the waitress? I'm paying."

At first I thought he must be offering to order something more for me, even though we had just finished a big meal with two bottles of wine. But in Marcel's dark eyes I saw another kind of hunger.

He said, "These girls are very nice, and it is safe."

When we first entered the roadhouse, I saw the woman owner exchange charged looks with Marcel as she greeted the two of us warmly. Now it was clear to me: he wanted to lay her and was suggesting that I might like the pretty little white-aproned waitress who had served us.

"No, thanks," I said, attempting to give the impression that a little strange love after lunch was as commonplace to me as it appeared to be to Marcel Savoie. "I gotta get on and pick up the cement or I'll be late getting back to camp, and besides, I'm afraid of getting a dose of *chau piss*."

The waitress gave me a dirty look. Marcel didn't look too happy either; he was going to miss out on laying the proprietress.

The next day Marcel insisted that I accompany him to his house to meet his mother and have something to drink.

What in the hell does he want me to meet his mother for? I wondered, as I looked him over for any signs of his intention. I was Johnny Bananas from the Brooklyn ghetto, a GI who had somehow managed to survive three years of war in Europe. My forte was definitely not meeting women for tea at nine in the morning.

"Thanks, Marcel, but I better not. I was sent here to get this furniture factory on line, and there's a lot to be done," I hedged.

But Marcel was not to be put off.

"I have told my mother about you," he said, "and she wants to meet you very much."

The war had been one adventure after another to date, so why not follow Marcel and see what was up?

Marcel directed me to park the army truck in front of a great house that overlooked the city and lead me into the garage where Monsieur Savoie's French car—kept safe and in good working order during the long years of deprivation—was parked. The garage was grander than most people's homes with white tile wainscotting and wonderful old paintings on the walls. I stopped to look and remarked on the richness and beauty around me.

Then Marcel led me into the dining room where his mother and father were having their after-breakfast coffee at a massive table that would accommodate at least thirty people. The furniture was all hand-carved and the walls were enriched with paintings.

I shook hands with Monsieur Savoie, and he introduced me to his stunning wife who was wearing a long satin dressing gown. She was a tall woman with reddish-blond hair and blue eyes—quite unlike her son who was short with curly black hair and dark eyes. (As a matter of fact, Marcel did not look like either his father or mother, who were both typical Germanic types.) But what surprised me most was the age difference between the parents. Madame Savoie, the most astonishingly beautiful woman I had ever seen, was at least thirty years younger than her husband.

Absolutely puzzled as to why I was here, I followed Marcel obediently into the adjoining room where he poured me a large snifter of Pernod with a cognac chaser. I was seated facing his mother through the archway, his father's back toward me. Madame kept looking over Monsieur's shoulder at me, smiling. As I sipped slowly, I kept thinking, "What is this assignment? Why am I here? The furniture factory doesn't seem to have anything to do with the Army. My sitting here early in the morning downing alcohol doesn't seem to have anything to do with the Army. And Madame—is she giving me the eye?"

From time to time Marcel disappeared, leaving me alone in this sumptuous room surrounded by tall cabinets of carved cherry with beveled glass doors that revealed hundreds of bottles of liquor of every kind. Madame and Monsieur were talking in low voices, and I got the definite feeling that they were discussing me. "What in the hell is going on?" I thought to myself. "This cannot possibly be happening."

Marcel reappeared and asked me if I wanted another drink.

"No, thanks," I replied. "That's all I can handle. I've got to drive, you know."

Madame and Monsieur stood up to bid me goodbye. I shook his hand formally. When I put out my hand toward Madame, she grasped it with both of hers, giving it a meaningful squeeze before she drew away.

That afternoon Marcel and I drove to Holland to pick up materials for the factory. Next morning when I appeared at the plant, Marcel greeted me saying, "Let's go."

"OK. What are we gonna do today?"

"We have to go to my house again."

"Do you have to pick something up there?" I said. "Did you forget something?"

By now we were driving down the street, and we went for a

185

couple of blocks before he answered, "*Voulez-vous* fuck *ma mere?*"

I was so surprised that I couldn't speak for twenty or thirty seconds. Finally I found my voice. "Marcel do you know what you're saying? Do you know what "fuck" means?"

"Yes, I do," he replied in French. "My mother wants you to go to bed with her."

I had seen little boys and girls pimping for their sisters and mothers, but I just couldn't fathom this sophisticated young man offering me his aristocratic mother.

"What about your father, Marcel?" I said. "And I've got a wife back home. One of these days I'm gonna go back."

"Don't worry about my father. It's OK. No problem," he said emphatically, easing, somewhat, my apprehension at even *thinking* about bedding his mother. "My mother wants you," he repeated.

The temptation was too great. I had been away for three years, and Madame Savoie was very, very attractive. "Shit," I thought to myself, "I don't even know if I'm gonna make it home." And, besides, I had the blessing of the husband and son. Within two blocks of the family chateau, I made up my mind to go to bed with her. It was hard to imagine Johnny Bananas, the kid who went without so much in Brooklyn, was now being wined and dined in Europe and even offered the favors of an upper-class woman.

"What are you gonna do, Marcel?" I asked, still a little reluctant and wondering what the hell was really going on. Would he be wandering around the house while I was in bed with his mother?

"Oh, *Jean*, I will be downstairs in bed with the maid," he assured me. "Don't worry. No problem."

Madame greeted me in the salon and poured me another snifter of Pernod, which, I was to learn later, contained absinthe. Made from wormwood and herbs, absinthe has a very high alcohol content with mind-altering properties, which caused it to be outlawed in the States.

"Marcel tells me you are married," she said as we slowly sipped our drinks.

"Yes," I admitted.

"How long has it been since you saw your wife?"

"Almost three years," I said. "My wife has never seen me in a soldier's uniform."

"Haven't you been home on compassionate leave?"

"The American army is the only one which does not have any kind of leave to return home during wartime. And when this is over,

I'll be going to Japan," I said, feeling a little sorry for myself.

"It doesn't seem right," she said, obviously feeling sorry for me, too. "Husbands and wives should not be separated for that long. And do you have children?"

"No, no children, Madame. And you?" I asked. "Do you have any children besides Marcel?"

"Yes, we have a daughter who attends a boarding school in Antwerp," she answered.

But there was something beyond concern for our families that Madame and I were feeling as we went up the grand curving stairway to her bedroom. I had never seen anything like that luxurious room except in the movies. The great square bathtub encased in marble was a far cry from a makeshift GI shower, and the huge bed with down comforters was certainly an improvement over the GI cot.

"What would your wife think if she knew this?" Madame asked, sitting on the edge of the bath as I luxuriated in the bubbles and hot water.

"She's not gonna find out," I replied.

"*C'est la guerre,*" she said letting her gown slip from her shoulders as I dried myself with the warm towel.

"And what about your husband?" I asked, still a little unsure.

"He is an old man, *Jean,* and he does not care." she assured me.

"You are a beautiful woman, Madame," I whispered, drawing her toward me.

"I am not *Madame, Jean.* My name is Claudette."

And then the thoughts of spouses and war faded away, and there were only two people in the whole world. Johnny Bananas and Claudette.

Time was non-existent in that Belgian boudoir, and it was well past noon before our passion was spent.

"Do you want to see me again?" Claudette asked as we paused for a last embrace before descending the stairs.

Of course, I wanted to see her again, but for her to want to see me again set my head awhirl. "*Oui, oui,*" I said breathlessly. "When?"

"Tomorrow?"

Still obsessed with work, I said, "It's not for me to say when. I work for you and am at your disposal."

"I want to see you again, *mon cheri,* and soon. Work is not important and we had a wonderful time today," she whispered.

My head was swimming with thoughts of seeing her again when I returned to my unit that evening.

"How's the new job going?" Jerry asked.

"Great," I said.

"Just what do you do?"

"Oh, I drive a 6 X 6 and haul material for this furniture company. And I translate."

There was no way I was going to tell Jerry or anyone else what was really going on in my new assignment and have them spoil things for me.

The next morning after I greeted Marcel, I sheepishly turned to Monsieur Savoie. When he smiled and warmly shook my hand, I felt reassured that he wasn't about to shoot me.

"Your family is Italian," he said. "Are you a Chicago gangster?"

"No." I replied.

"Then you must be a cowboy. The cinemas always portray Americans as one or the other."

"I work in the forest industry. It is hard work. A man must be very strong."

"Have you met any Belgian women beside my wife? They are known for their beauty and their passion, you know."

It still hadn't completely dawned on me that he knew about my liaison with his wife. Where was this all leading?

Monsieur waved us off cheerily as we left the factory for my day's assignment. I didn't mention my impending assignation to Marcel. I wanted to see if his mother had actually meant what she said.

"Well, where to today, Marcel?" I asked brightly.

He looked askance at me and said, "To my house, of course. Don't you remember?"

"Yes, I remember. I just wanted to make sure I wasn't dreaming," I sighed.

"My mother likes you," he assured me.

This was the second day of what came to be a daily assignment. Claudette and I began each visit with a snifter of Pernod which I drank sparingly, not wanting to be oblivious to the delights of the boudoir. She was starved for intimacy and responded affectionately to my advances, but our morning encounters were strictly sexual. There was never any thought that we would see each other socially. Her evenings and parties were reserved for other people and other times.

I was young and strong. The war and my illness had made me thin and serious-looking, but I was always clean-shaven and neat. Even some of the light and laughter that had been lost through

188

hardship, reappeared in my blue eyes.

"Why have you chosen me—an American GI?" I asked her the second day.

"Because, *mon cheri,* you will go back to America and not tell anyone there, and since you do not socialize here, you will not tell anyone here," she replied.

After lovemaking, we always went down to meet Marcel for a scrumptious lunch of Belgian endive salad, steak or eggs, *pomme frites,* and crepes. I knew the steak and eggs were only available on the black market and atrociously expensive, and I just couldn't believe that I was living this high. I finally had it made.

Each afternoon we went to pick up material for the factory. Early on in the job Marcel announced that his father needed petrol for his car and asked me to get him some. I arranged to have him pick up six of the eight Jerry cans that were filled and carried on the running board of the truck each morning. My reasoning, which was ridiculous, was that I was absolved from the stealing since I did not give it to them, but just turned my head.

When Marcel offered to lend me a thousand francs and assured me that I needn't worry about paying it back, I realized that I was involved in black market gasoline. I took a couple of thousand francs, but with considerable misgivings, and then Marcel began giving me bottles of liquor. I could accept the liquor more readily than the cash: I shared it with my buddies. However, as time went on, I began to suspect that there was something subversive in what I was doing. Here I was being showered with sex and money and liquor to keep me from exposing what was going on. Since I was sent to the job by my company commander, I felt that by offering him some of the booze, I would incriminate him also.

When he accepted it willingly, agreeing to store some for me in his foot locker, I felt relieved that I was not alone in this intrigue. It was another relief to me when I noticed a German burp gun in his footlocker. We GIs had had to surrender ours, but he had kept his illegal booty.

After a couple of months of this unbelievable detail, the war with Germany came to an end. That May night the streets of Herstal and Liège were alive with celebrants who happily called out "Liberator" to GIs as they passed. The cafes were crowded and the Belgians wore their best clothes, but, otherwise, there was not the tumultuous celebration that we were later to learn took place in the States. Since the Germans had been driven from their country some months earlier, the Belgians were well on their way to normalization, and this final surrender of the Germans was merely the icing on the cake.

The next morning we were told there would be no work detail that day because we all had to attend the movie "Two Down and One To Go." Italy and Germany were vanquished, but Japan was still ahead.

"Come on," I said to Turk Thompson, "I can't phone the people I've been working for, so I have to drive over and tell them that I won't be in today."

Turk's eyes lit up when we arrived at the stately chateau. "You've been working here?" he said.

"Well, not exactly. I'll tell you later," I said as Marcel answered the door.

"You are early, John," he greeted me, inviting us both in for a drink.

"Yes, well, I can't work today because we all have to see a movie,"

Claudette floated down the stairs in a new pink sleeping ensemble that made her look more elegant than ever. Turk gasped, and I knew he must be thinking "What the hell is this?"

"What is it, *Jean?*" she inquired, obviously distressed. "Are you going back home?"

"No. Madame. It's just that I can't work today, but I surely will not be going back home. We still have the war with Japan to win," I said, addressing her formally so Turk wouldn't get suspicious.

Marcel poured us a generous Pernod and cognac chaser in the salon. Claudette came and stood close behind my chair placing her hands affectionately on my shoulders, drawing me near to her. I saw the look on Turk's face as he dipped his head down close to his snifter, looking slyly up at me as if to say, "Why, you son-of-a-bitch. You're laying her, aren't you?"

Marcel continued to pour drink after drink. By the time we left, Turk and I were pretty well bombed.

"I'll see you in the morning," I promised as we all shook hands in the foyer.

Back in the truck, Turk could hardly wait to begin questioning me. "You bastard! You're screwing her, aren't you?"

"No, I'm not," I lied.

"Well, I think you are," he insisted. "It looks to me like you are more than just friends."

I denied everything, but by the time we arrived back at camp he still was not convinced.

Even though the war with Germany was over, my work detail continued and I resumed my daily routine at the factory *and* the chateau. I still had the feeling that I was involved in something more than appeared to the eye, but I couldn't figure out what.

Arriving at the factory one morning in early June, Marcel greeted me with the news that we had to go to the railroad yard right away. "We have a big job to do," he said.

"What's the big deal?" I said.

"You'll see," he replied happily. "You'll see."

Well, I *saw* all right. At the station there were eighteen rickety box cars guarded by GI sentries. These old wagons called "forty and eight" had been designed to carry either forty troops or eight horses to the front during World War I. When Marcel opened one of the doors, my eyes all but popped out of my head. There shining dimly in the darkness of the car were hundreds of silver ingots, an incredible treasure, the likes of which I had never seen. I recalled seeing picture of such ingots stacked on Philadelphia or New York docks when nations made their payments to each other—but to actually come in contact with such wealth was quite overwhelming.

I stared incredulously at Marcel as he explained, "There is this much silver in all eighteen of the cars. We have to move it to the warehouse at the furniture factory."

Still somewhat stunned at the sight, I tried to pick up a bar, but could only lift one end.

"Who's gonna move this stuff?" I gasped, realizing what a big operation it was going to be and still not fully aware of what was happening.

"*You* are going to move it, Johnny, and you can have all of it you want."

My head was swimming. There had to be big people, important people, involved in this operation I was sure—men as high as generals, maybe. "Shit," I blurted out, "I can hardly lift one end of these goddam things let alone move them to the warehouse. I've gotta go back and talk with the colonel and see if I can get help."

Back at base section headquarters, I reported my dilemma to the colonel. "There's something funny going on with all those carloads of silver," I said, not dreaming that he might be involved.

"Who are you?" He looked at me as if he had never seen me before.

It took a couple of minutes for the realization to sink in that this guy knew perfectly well who I was and what was going on. He had

191

assumed I would go along with the heist, and now that I was questioning it, he pretended not to know me. Without further acknowledgement by either of us, I turned around and left. I reported to Captain Dixon and explained that there was an illegal operation underway. The next morning he and I went back to see.

At the factory we found about twenty Italian prisoners, guarded by American sentries, neatly stacking the silver bars in the warehouse. Looking closely at the ingots, we discovered bronze plaques which indicated the origin of the treasure was French Indochina. The silver had been consigned to Deutsch Bank in Hanover. It would have required high-ranking army officials to arrange for its shipment by rail to the factory here in Herstal.

Marcel was nowhere to be seen, and the sentries did not challenge Captain Dixon and me. I suppose we could have had the Italian prisoners load our command car with silver and no one would have attempted to stop us. Instead, I spoke with a couple of the prisoners in Italian. "You're working very hard. The silver is heavy."

"We've been working all night," they said. "We're tired but we're almost finished now. Are you Italian?"

"Yes, my family came from Italy, but I am an American," I answered. Turning to Captain Dixon I said, "Well, what do you think of this operation?"

"Christ!" he exclaimed, "this is a king's ransom! Let's get out of here, and I'll talk with our commander, Colonel Clifford."

Colonel Clifford went to inspect the silver operation at the warehouse and also determined there was something crooked going on. When he went to base section to clarify the matter, he was told to "back off and forget the whole thing." We assumed that the big wheels running this enterprise were probably generals at either end.

And that ended the best tour of duty I had in the army. No more crepes; no more Pernod; and no more clandestine meetings with Claudette. All that remained were fond memories of what seemed to be a dream, dreamed near the end of a war.

Preparation for the Asiatic Theater and End of the War in Japan

It was the Fourth of July when I reported to the 1143rd Engineer Combat Group at Laon, about fifteen miles from Rheims. I was very depressed that I had been chosen from among the thousands of other GIs to remain in Europe to prepare for ending the war in Japan.

192

I was thinking about many of my friends who had already headed back to the States as Major Ross outlined my duties. I was to run a sawmill to cut lumber for crating machinery headed for Japan. "You'll have fifty German prisoners working for you," he said, "and they will be guarded by liberated Poles who the Germans used in forced labor to build the West Wall. They'll have German rifles to give the prisoners a taste of their own medicine, if necessary. By the way," he continued, "there are some people here who know you."

"Who," I asked eagerly thinking maybe Walt or some of the other fellows I had been separated from were around.

"Captain Colyer and Colonel Clifford," he reported smartly. "You do know them, don't you?"

"I sure as hell do," I replied, my mind spinning with thoughts that those two bastards must be the reason I was chosen to stay on Europe. They both knew me and knew my work.

That night when I ran into Colyer he greeted me with, "Hi, Johnny! How are you?"

"I'm pissed off! That's how I am. I think you are responsible for this assignment. The rest of them are going home, and I'm still sitting here, headed for Japan," I said angrily as the captain turned and walked away.

There was nothing to be done, of course, but get on with the work, so I found myself supervising a crew of German POWs at a portable sawmill that had been made in Corinth, Mississippi. Two of the older prisoners ran my mobile machine shop, and since there wasn't a lot of repair to be done, one afternoon they were making souvenirs from a German airplane propellor. Paul was busy making me a ring when all the commotion and hollering began, and hearing a shot, I ran out of the shop and saw a German prisoner lying dead on the ground.

The only reason a Pole could shoot a prisoner was if he was trying to escape, and this guy was running toward the woods and did not heed the guard's warning to stop. The German translator told me that the dead man was headed for the toilet when he was shot, but that is doubtful since he was more than a hundred feet beyond the slit trench.

I shook my head in disbelief that he would try to escape. The machinery for repatriating the Germans was already in motion, and if he had only waited, he would have made it safely home. The war was over for him, but it wasn't over for me—not until the bomb was dropped on Japan.

But still no orders to go home! After three-and-a-half years overseas, I had come to the end of my rope. I meant to return to Doris and the Pacific Northwest no matter what the consequences. I was hitchhiking to Rheims when Colonel Clifford came along and picked me up.

"Where are you going, John?" he said as I climbed into his command car.

"I'm not going to work anymore, and I'm headed into base section headquarters to find why I haven't received orders to go back to the States," I said. "I feel I've done my share in this thing. You can put me in jail or whatever you want to do with me, but I'm not going to work anymore." I was feeling as determined as when I had told the local policeman to put me in jail, if he had to, but I would not stop cutting wood.

When we reached the colonel's office, he called in Major Ross and asked him to take me to Rheims and make sure that I got on the next orders that were cut to go home. As it turned out, their intervention was not necessary. My name was on the orders that had been cut that morning. I was on my way home!

Back in my room, I announced to the two German prisoners who were my orderlies that I was going back to the states. One of the men pointed to a map on the wall and asked where I lived. I showed him, and he asked "California?" apparently the only state that he knew of.

"No," I said, emptying my barracks bag as I spoke, "north of California." I gave them some candy bars, and perhaps it was this gesture or perhaps it was the fact that I was going home and they were not that caused one of the men to cry.

My heart went out to them, and I assured them in my broken German that they would be going home soon, too.

An Eternity in Marseilles

On the train to Marseilles, we were pensive. What were we going to find when we got home? Would it all be the same or would things have changed? We had all been away so long and had seen so much tragedy that we were, even now, apprehensive whether we would make it home or not. And, indeed, two men were killed on that very train trip. One was hanging out too far from the train step and hit the side of a tunnel. The other stepped in front of a "galloping goose" that sped past us while we were stopped. Then—if and when we got on our homeward ship—there was the possibility of being sunk by drifting mines.

Our ship was not in port, and we did not know when it would arrive, so everything was in a pattern of "wait and hope." Miraculously, my old buddy Walt Cramoga turned out to be in a tent next to me, so we commiserated and waited over beer at the local cafe.

And then the day we had been dreaming of for nearly four years arrived. We headed for the dock, still holding our breath for fear something would keep us from our appointment. And sure enough, winding down one of the narrow streets, our truck had to slow almost to a stop behind forty or fifty people plodding along behind a horse-drawn hearse. The rickety cart bearing the corpse didn't look as though it could make it to the cemetery.

"You know, that's a bad omen," I said to the guy next to me. My intuition told me that something was going to happen, and we were not going to get on the boat.

And sure as hell, when we arrived on the dock, there was no ship.

But the next day it was there, proud as could be. A Victory ship named the *Marine Raven*, and I was on my way!

11

Home At Last

Doris is Waiting

I hitchhiked west from Mount Vernon to Anacortes and home. Mr. and Mrs. Kack, who knew Doris and her family, picked me up and offered to take me right to my door.

The Skagit Flats were a blur as we drove along—not because of our speed but because of the turbulence in my head and my heart. I was overwhelmingly grateful to be alive, my head spinning at the thought of seeing Doris.

We crossed the Swinomish Slough bridge to Fidalgo Island, and as my anticipation increased, the car speed decreased—or so it seemed. The road through Summit Park dragged on and on for what felt like twenty miles instead of the two that it actually was. But, at last, we arrived at Deans' Corner with the small service station and grocery store just as I remembered them. Only four miles to go!

"How could the road have lengthened like this?" I agonized, as we wound interminably along the shoreline of Fidalgo Bay, past the railroad trestle and Weaverling Spit, and crept slowly up the hill south of town.

At the crest of the rise, Anacortes spread out before us. The stores, the mills, the houses, and one of those houses was mine! A few more blocks down Commercial Avenue, up twenty-second street, a right on N Avenue and I was home! Home, at last!

I fear I did not say "Goodbye" or "Thank you" to the Kacks as I tumbled out of the car because Doris had flung open the door and was waiting for me on the porch. She was more beautiful than I remembered—her face sweeter, more mature. All of the suffering and loneliness of the past four years seemed to cancel itself out as we fell into each other's arms.

That night I lay awake long after Doris had fallen asleep, and though I could see the stars through the holes in our roof, I felt like the richest man alive.

The next morning when I walked down to the police station, who should be on duty but Marvin Beebe, the cop who had confiscated my rifles the day after Pearl Harbor. His back was toward me as I entered the office, and when he turned around, his face blanched.

"I've come for my rifles and ammunition," I said, staring at him contemptuously.

"What now?" he said, apparently shocked and stalling for time. Surely he'd heard me.

"I want my guns and shells back."

"You've been gone a long time."

"I want my rifles and ammunition," I repeated, unwilling to make small talk.

As he gave me my rifles, he noted that much of the ammunition was missing because several local men who had not gone to war had used my guns and shells to hunt deer in my absence. I was still angry at having been thought a danger to my country when I had been more willing than my detractors to fight for her. But I knew the war had made me stronger, too. I had learned many engineering skills, I'd come to appreciate home and family more than ever, and I'd made peace with myself over my Italian heritage.

On my way home that day, rifles in hand, I remembered the morning I woke in my fox hole to find, overhead, a cross hung with a set of dog tags and the sign "Dago John. RIP." I smiled to myself, recalling the good-natured sniggering of my buddies who had pulled the joke, and I knew that from that time on Dago John would truly "Rest in Peace."

EPILOGUE

I decided it would take too long for me to go back to school to earn a degree, so I continued my education after the war by reading and doing. I left the timber industry for the salmon industry, where I became a foreman and head machinist. As the years passed, I became more proficient with mechanical equipment and went to work for Shell Oil Company as a machinist. This job developed into foreman, then supervisor of mechanical equipment and consultant to other Shell locations in the United States.

After we finished our house and things were going well for us, Doris and I decided to share with others and help in any way we could. We worked with scouting and veterans' groups and often paid the grocery or milk bills for families that could not pay themselves. When we retired, we became full-time volunteers, happy to do anything we could for the community.

The morning the invitation from the White House arrived, I thought it was just another piece of junk mail and put it aside to be thrown in the trash. Something special about the letter must have caught my eye, however, and made me open it.

The White House   April 12, 1985
Washington, D.C.
Dear Mr. Tursi:

As you may know, April 22nd-28th has been declared national volunteer week. During this week the President will be participating in a number of activities honoring outstanding volunteers and voluntary organizations.

On behalf of President Reagan, I would like to invite you to join him for a Rose Garden ceremony honoring outstanding senior volunteers from the Retired Senior Volunteer Program on Friday April 26, 1985.

You should plan to arrive no later than 10:15 am at east visitor's entrance on east Executive Avenue with photo identification. Please RSVP to the office of Private Sector Initiatives by April 18th with your date of birth and social security number if you plan to attend.

We look forward to seeing you on the 26th.

Sincerely,
Frederick J. Ryan
Director Private Sector Initiative

I had been chosen for this honor because my volunteer involvement with the community was so varied: everything from translating for non-English-speaking patients at the local hospital to construction of exhibit rooms at two local museums. Doris and I also showed slides of our world travels to local senior and religious groups, and we transported sick people to doctors and hospitals in the northwest part of the state.

It was with a great deal of gratitude and humility that Doris and I entered the Rose Garden that cloudless spring morning. My life which had begun in poverty on the edges of crime, moved to the forests and waters of the Pacific Northwest, taken me to Europe in World War II and back home, now culminated in this honor. Truly it had been a long journey to the Rose Garden.